Advance Praise for the Book

In this interactive book of daily meditations, author and Spirit speak to each other in a sort of call and response rhythm, and the reader is challenged to focus on a particular theme for the day. Some entries include an "Evening Reflection" that offers a review of how the events in the author's day echo the teaching of the day. The resulting intimacy and guidance of a gentle and enticing kind provide an invitation to live deeply and quietly, inwardly and purposefully. Many people will surely feel inspired and empowered by this special book, which is full of deep, candid, and honest soul-searching that awakens one's own deepest needs and aspirations.
– **Matthew Fox**, spiritual theologian, Episcopal priest, activist, former member of the Dominican order, and author of 35 books, including *Original Blessing*

In this book of gentle meditations on navigating life's journey with depth and grace, inspirational author David Sharp offers a deep breath for our souls. His wisdom is simple and expansive, his language clear and inviting.
– **Mirabai Starr**, author of *God of Love* and *Caravan of No Despair*, speaker, leading voice in the emerging interspiritual movement, and translator of the mystics. www.mirabaistarr.com

Acting and life are collaborative arts. As a performing artist it is of utmost importance to be in collaborative harmony with the director. The best directors don't make you "do" things – they help you make your own discoveries. Dr. David Preston Sharp's *Power for Life* is a book about being an active participant and mindful collaborator with the best and (most subtly obvious) director in our life – the Universal Divine One (of many earthly names).

It's also a "how-to" book about being here now; about "ask and you shall receive", and "knock and the door shall be opened." It's a book about listening with open ears, open eyes, open mind, and open heart. It is a book about living artfully.

And like a good director, it doesn't tell you what to do or how to do it, but guides by gentle suggestion, leaving the deepest and most profound answers for you to discover on your own.
– **Brian Stokes Mitchell**, American stage, film, and television actor and singer, winner of the 2000 Tony award for Best Actor in a Musical (*Kiss Me, Kate*)

DAVID SHARP

Power for Life

INSPIRATIONAL GUIDANCE FOR DAILY LIVING

WOOD LAKE

Editor: Ellen Turnbull
Proofreader: Dianne Greenslade
Designer: Robert MacDonald

Library and Archives Canada Cataloguing in Publication
Title: Power for life : inspirational guidance for
daily living / David Sharp.
Names: Sharp, David (David Preston), author.
Identifiers: Canadiana (print) 20190046708 | Canadiana
(ebook) 20190046724 | ISBN 9781773431598 (softcover)
| ISBN 9781773431420 (ebook)
Subjects: LCSH: Devotional literature. | LCSH: Christian life
– Meditations.
Classification: LCC BV4832.3 .S53 2019 | DDC 242/.2–dc23

ISBN 978-1-77343-159-8

Published by Wood Lake Publishing Inc.
485 Beaver Lake Road, Kelowna, BC, Canada V4V 1S5
www.woodlake.com | 250.766.2778

Wood Lake Publishing acknowledges the financial support
of the Government of Canada. Wood Lake Publishing
acknowledges the financial support of the Province of
British Columbia through the Book Publishing Tax Credit.

Wood Lake Publishing would like to acknowledge that we
operate in the unceded territory of the Syilx/Okanagan
People, and we work to support reconciliation and
challenge the legacies of colonialism. The Syilx/Okanagan
territory is a diverse and beautiful landscape of deserts
and lakes, alpine forests and endangered grasslands.
We honour the ancestral stewardship of the
Sylix/Okanagan People.

GOLD

Printed in Canada.
Printing 10 9 8 7 6 5 4 3 2 1

DEDICATION

To my parents, Rev. John D. Sharp and Annie R. Sharp,
who are my original daily guidance providers.

And to all who endeavour to grow ever more deeply
into their spiritual potential.

Acknowledgements

I want to thank my wife, Jeannine Goode-Allen. This book would not exist without her inspiration and encouragement. She introduced this practice to me and noticed that my guidance came through in poetic form. It was she who encouraged me to keep each day's guidance and write an evening reflection.

I want to thank Michael Schwartzentruber, editor at Wood Lake Publishing. Even though he was not soliciting manuscripts at the time, he looked at my sample anyway. Without his willingness to check out my work, this book might still be sitting on the desk.

I am indebted to my editor, Ellen Turnbull, whose opinions, suggested revisions, and overall guidance tightened my words and reduced the fluff so that my thoughts have more clarity and my words read more smoothly.

I also offer thanks to the following family members:
• my late father, Rev. John Dell Sharp, who as both Dad and Presbyterian minister gave me insight into the importance of spiritual guidance;
• my mother, Annie Ruth Sharp, who inspired my love for writing and fostered an understanding of the power of words;
• my daughter Danea Sharp, with whom I first shared many of the pieces and who offered personal affirmation of their usefulness;
• my son Justin Sharp, who helped me understand that guiding others with integrity means I must always stay open to guidance myself;
• my daughter Alicia Goode-Allen and my son Joshua Goode-Allen, who were daily test subjects (unbeknownst to them), as they were living at home at the time of writing.

Finally, I am grateful to those writers whose daily guidance books have helped and inspired me. They made me want to grow enough to write one myself one day in the hope of helping and inspiring others. Well, one day has become this book, thanks to Wood Lake Publishing.

INTRODUCTION

This book is the fruit of meditation, contemplation, and deep listening.

The motivation was my desire to deepen my communion with God and grow in spiritual maturity. My wife, Dr. Jeannine Goode-Allen, introduced me to the practice that I have used for this book. We would write a question with our right hand and take time to receive an answer, which we would write out with our left hand. The right hand accesses the intellectual left side of the brain, and the left hand accesses the more intuitive right side. After a couple of weeks of doing this together, Jeannine noticed that my responses sounded like poems. She encouraged me to start collecting them. She also suggested that I write an evening reflection to assess how I did with living the day's guidance. I did not know these would become a book when I began the practice, as that was not my goal.

As I continued the practice solo, I began to discern how to place the words on the page, which is why it looks like poetry. The discipline of right hand/left hand allowed the more controlling aspects of my mind to loosen. I was able to journey inward to a place where Spirit's guidance was clearly heard. The more I engaged in this practice, the more sensitive I became to Spirit's *voice* within me. I could feel the difference between the voice of Spirit coming through and my own thinking voice trying to manipulate the guidance. Though I have been doing this practice for years now, I still experience wonder and awe each time I receive a guidance.

Qualities such as joy, patience, kindness, goodness, gentleness, faithfulness, and self-control are hallmarks of spiritual maturity. Each guidance speaks in some way to their development, and challenges us to become more aware of ourselves and what we send into the world through our words and actions. Daily living can challenge our commitment and resolve to be loving and peaceful. The goal of this work is to inspire enduring changes in behaviour.

Each daily guidance is meant to be sipped into the soul. I suggest that each line be read slowly. Allow it to seep into your being. It does not matter how long or short each guidance may be. I have found that they all contain rich messages that fill the spirit and provide inspiration for personal and spiritual growth. Try reading the guidance several times during the day to remind yourself of its directive and to see how you are doing with it as the day unfolds. The Evening Reflections scattered throughout the book, where I share my experiences and insights, are meant to be supportive and helpful.

There is no single way to grow and mature as a spiritual being. One person can make a huge jump in an instant due to prevailing circumstances and past experience, while another can take a more measured approach of slow and steady growth. This book adopts the slow and steady approach, with each guidance connected to the day before. You might think of them as cuts on a diamond. Each one sparkles on its own, even if the directive in one seems close to that of another. As you take in these daily readings, I encourage you to become aware of what seems to be staying with you from previous days. It may well be that you do not remember anything specific, but that you feel a general improvement or growth in your spiritual awareness, outlook, manner, and demeanour.

That is what happened to me. Of course, there were many challenges. And there were days I was less than successful at living the guidance. Sometimes I decided to live a guidance again the next day; and there were a few I decided I needed to live for one or two weeks before I felt I could move on. Several became such favourites that I

printed them and put them on my office bulletin board. More times than not, I made a copy of the daily guidance and carried in my pocket, to pull out when I felt the need to remind myself of its specific focus. This was an especially useful and powerful habit, and one that I encourage you to adopt. I even read many of them to friends and acquaintances when I sensed it was helpful, or, to be more accurate, when Spirit guided me to read them aloud to others.

Don't feel restricted to reading one guidance per day every day. Feel free to read several at a time, or read the whole thing as a book and then go back and live each day. You may feel like staying with a particular guidance for more than one day. That is fine. They all work together and there is no one right way to use them.

I hope you enjoy journeying with these potent words and messages. Even the ones that sound easy to live into can prove challenging in ways that are humbling. But humility is the great tool of spiritual growth. And as pleasing as each day's piece may be to look at and read, they are all about growth, which means they are about doing our work. However, they are also about grace. And when work and grace come together, transformation can be expected.

Are you ready?

You must be, for if the book is in your hands it is out of mine. May God guide us all!

DAY 1

God, what would you have me say and do today?

You have begun well...
by asking.

Continue to ask today,
in each encounter, event, and circumstance.

It takes only a moment's intent.

Divine communication is much quicker than
human thought or words spoken.

Feel my answers within you.

Today we will dance.
You move...
   I move...
      We move...
together.

So keep asking,
and watch the dance unfold –
each step revealed
and taken easily and joyfully,
      even the difficult ones.

Ask and dance.
Ready?

EVENING REFLECTION

It has been my experience that sensing and follow-ing subtle direction from deep within yields a far better outcome than going with my own thinking. Even if I cannot really know what the outcome would have been had I chosen a different action, I do know when I have followed the inner leading. And it is there, in that space, that life asks, *Do you want to dance*?

Dancing is a partnership. Even dancing alone is usu-ally in relationship with music. In terms of dancing with Spirit, the question is, *Do I want to live in rela-tionship with Spirit, or try to do it all myself*?

I can feel the difference when Spirit emanates from within. There is an excitement that comes from rec-ognizing the living, person-specific guidance of God. When I feel the excitement born of that recognition, I know it is wise go with it. I don't have to, of course, but there is a reason for this inner excitement. I have had many experiences of *not* going with the feeling in my gut and having things not work out that other-wise may have – if I had just followed my gut. (I have come to understand my gut as *God-Using-Tummy* to get me a message.)

How was your dance with Spirit today?

DAY 2

God, what would you have me say and do today?

Say *I love you*
   with your eyes,
   your words,
     your heart,
     and your actions.

     No matter what you are
     really feeling,
   say and think,
I love you anyway.

That is all you need to do today.
The rest will come.

   Will you do this?
     Today?
       All day?

EVENING REFLECTION

To think, say, and show *I love you* all the time? Now, if everyone could do that, I think it would be a different world. To spend even a day living this is quite the challenge. To spend days, or weeks, or years living out just this guidance would be enough to take one to the highest heights of maturity and spiritual growth.

But this guidance is for a day. It is practice.

How did you do?

DAY 3

God, what do you want me to say and do today?

Let life come to you.
   Don't press.

Allow everyone to be where they are
and the way they are today.

It is all right.
   Let it be okay today.

Allow the perfection of the day
to include the perfect imperfections.

Rest from all effort to change,
control, or manipulate.

It will be okay without your input.

   Just ride the day.
Relax.
Let things flow.

   And you?

   Just float along.
You will know what to say and do
   in each moment,

for I am along for the ride,
   whispering in your ear.

I hope you don't mind the company.

DAY 4

God, what would you have me say and do today?

Switch.
Switch from your thinking mind
to your divine heart.

You will speak differently
and think differently.
You will sound different
and feel different.

Stay in this dimension of your
consciousness all day.

When you notice you have
left your heart behind,
gently readjust.

Intellect, instinct, and all manner
of knowing are best served when
filtered through a heart aligned with me.

When this is done, wisdom flows.
Light shines on all,
rendering all holy and blessed.

Take on a Christ consciousness.
Become a true representation of my love.
Switch.
Open your divine heart
and watch what happens.

Those last lines about all being holy and blessed kind
of threw me.

Awful things happen all over our beautiful planet:
wars, freak accidents, terminal illnesses, and brazen
attacks on unsuspecting people. I know our world is
not all sweetness and light. It can be dangerous and
scary. So what of this light shining on all, rendering
it holy and blessed?

The genius of God is that God views all creation and
all things in it as holy. And, although it may be hard
for most of us to see, everything is ultimately blessed
and uplifted. This can only be because God works all
things for good, even the bad things, the tragic things,
the worst of the worst. In my experience, the worst
occurrences have at the very least taught me to appreciate when things are *not* at their worst; in other
words, I have learned to appreciate the goodness of
life and the good things in life.

The crazy thing is that we can experience the para-
dox of crying and laughing at the same time. We can
experience sadness and joy at the same time. We can
complain and count our blessings at the same time.
This is where I think the guidance is heading: Love
triumphs. Why? Because the presence of God is over
all.

If we connect to this truth and let it sink in, then we
grow to understand that there is nothing that is not
blessed. There is nothing that cannot bless and uplift
us, with God's help.

That is how great God is. That is how powerful divine
love is.

DAY 5

God, what would you have me do and say today?

Wait.
Pull back.

Do not dive off the cliff
into the ocean of attitude, judgment, and blame.

Hold off.
Make no move toward opinion.

Be stable in your mind;
allow light to shine through your eyes
and love to exude from
      head to foot.

This is your mission today, no matter what else
happens.

Let nothing deter you.

This effort will allow you to
uncover, access, and reside in the
divine.

And the divine will become the ever-deepening
ocean into which you may freely dive.
Blessings and grace await you there.

So today,
  wait.

Pull back. Be at peace.

DAY 6

God, what would you have me say and do today?

You know...
    Love.

Let love be the power
that takes you through
this day.

Think about the people you meet and
all the day's happenings as gifts for you.
Think of yourself as a gift for others.

If you find yourself straying from this
focus

    pause...
      stop...
        don't move.

Go into your soul's centre and find
that place of pure love.
  Let the love flow through your whole body.
Then
  move, speak, act.

Ahh,
the things you can do with love,
with joy, with graciousness,
with thankfulness to God!

DAY 7

God, what would you have me say and do today?

Give up.

Let go of holding on
to grudges, anger, or negative feelings.

Give up
    holding on to the force of ego
that only weakens your whole being.

Take a deep breath and let go.

Being able to do this is indicative of
your true nature and highest self.

Keep letting go, giving up,
releasing, and breathing out
        as negative energies
float away from you.

You will be tested in this,
so be strong in your commitment.
This is how spiritual growth happens.

As you let go of your darkness, you
will uncover my divine light
shining forth beauty,
kindness, joy,
    and love –
and waiting for you to shine forth today.

DAY 8

God, what would you have me say and do today?

Relax.
Just be.

No pressure to be a certain way.
    Just be alive
        and see with joyful awareness
the creation you are.

Notice your breathing.
Notice that you can see, feel, sense,
    taste, hear, touch.

Enjoy being today.
Feel
your aliveness:
    the gift of it,
    the privilege of it.

And be thankful.
Be thankful.

Be thankful.

DAY 9

God, what would you have of me today?

I would have all of you,
   in every way,
      at all times,
         always.

I already do, but the question is,
Do you realize it?

Even your doubts and disbeliefs about me are
part of the gift of free will that I have given as
a way of sharing myself with you.

I would have you give yourself back to me
daily
      as your gift to me.

In doing so, your consciousness has
a chance to grow and expand
      by leaps and bounds.

Will you give yourself to me today?

EVENING REFLECTION

Asking someone, "What would you have of me?" could
be considered an act of courage. It implies that you
are willing to do whatever is asked of you. Depending
on who you are saying this to, asking it of someone
can also be somewhat scary. In that I am asking this
of God, it becomes an act of trust and faith. I have
learned, however, that although the Divine may surprise, the Divine always loves. And love is compassionate and gentle; it never seeks to control, but to
guide one to be one's best self.

Christian scripture speaks of loving the Lord fully,
with all one's heart, soul, strength, and mind. This is
essentially our whole being. I am glad the One who
created me wants all of me – even while letting me
be me. It sounds convoluted, but it is, essentially,
what it means to be one with God.

DAY 10

God, what would you have me say and do today?

Follow my lead.
You will feel it in you.

Listen to your heart.
   You will hear me there.

Breathe deeply.
   I will fill you with inspiration,
      moment
         by
            moment.

I will show you the way today.
We will have fun, you and I.

Are you ready?
      Go!
Hey!
      Wait for me...

EVENING REFLECTION

God has a sense of humour.

Of course God does! Anything we can do, God can.
The Giver of All Life is the reason for all there is – all
creation and everything in it. (This does not mean it,
however, that God is the author of evil. All creation
is held in the field of divinity, but it does not mean it
is all OF God.)

God does have a sense of humour, and I have laughed
at God's jokes countless times. Sometimes, of course,
the joke is on me. This occurs when I am learning a
life lesson in a manner that is intense and uncomfortable, when I could have learned the same lesson
in a much easier way had I been wiser at the time.

God, I believe, loves to play with us and hear us
laugh. Joy, inspiration, fun, and laughter are not
antithetical to the Divine. When we finally got a
picture of Jesus laughing, we finally got it right.
God enjoys us!

But that is my experience. What's yours?

DAY 11

God, what would you have me say and do today?

Get quiet.
    Settle.
Let calm permeate
all you say and do.
    No rushing.
Be smooth and relaxed
in your movements.
    And listen.
Listen within the silence.
    Hear me.
Listen for me
in the depths of your soul.
    Let me sing my silence in you.
    Let me fill you with my rich offerings.
Receive my wisdom.

Walk the world today in silent calm.
Wonders await you!
    You'll see.

DAY 12

God, what would you have me say and do today?

Do to others
    what you would want done to yourself.
Talk to others
    the way you would want to be addressed.

This is a beautiful commitment.
    It asks that you look inside your heart
      and be honest about your actions.
    It demands compassion for others.
It is about oneness,
    and seeing yourself in others.

It is not easy.
It is also not so hard.

It is love in action.

Are you willing today?
Are you willing to be love?

DAY 13

God, what would you have me say and do today?

Speak with beauty.
Do all with grace.

Be like a poem that
    lifts the spirit and enlivens
        the heart.

Let your words flow
    like the refreshing waters
        of a bubbling stream,
        and let your actions
    drip with peace.

Let divine light emanate from your eyes.

Think,
    and allow love, kindness, and gentleness
        to guide your thoughts.

Watch...
as miracles unfold.

DAY 14

God, what would you have me say and do today?

Be patient.
    Wait.
Pause before saying or doing.

Waiting for you in that space
are guidance, encouragement, and the resources
to meet the needs of the day.
In that space
    you have the
opportunity to draw in
    wisdom, unconditional love,
        self-control, joy, peace,
            kindness, gentleness, and trust.

Today,
spend time in the spaces.
    They are wondrous places
        to visit.

Splash their blessings
all over you.

Okay, I know what you are thinking: the word "splash" came out of nowhere. Since there was not a single water reference in the guidance, where then did that come from?

It came from that primordial place where thought forms words. It is a creative way of expressing the idea that the blessings offered in the spaces created by patience and waiting flow over you.

The Divine is nothing if not creative. There is never just one way to get an idea across. I always did like the thought of tasting with my ears or touching with my eyes.

As far as patience goes, one of my favourite sermons preached by my father was on patience. The words, "But let patience have her perfect work" (James 1:4 KJV) still echo in my head. Patience is a quality that many find difficult to achieve. And now, when technology allows *instant* and *faster*, it is perhaps even more challenging to be patient.

That being said, spending a day practicing patience can yield amazing results. Patience takes the pressure off – everything. If you want to improve your ability to be patient and live its gifts, try this when you are feeling pressured: Inhale deeply, and as you exhale, let go of the need to control. Practice this for a day, and if it goes well see if you can stretch it over a couple of days. Any amount of patience is beneficial in our fast-paced society.

Patience doesn't keep us from accomplishing, it allows us to *enjoy* accomplishing. Or even to enjoy *not* accomplishing. Now that is an accomplishment!

DAY 15

God, what would you have me do and say today?

Be a mirror image of me.

I am you.
 You represent me in the world.

Be that which you cannot be
 when apart from me.

Today, hold me within you...
 Fall back into me
 when your ego pushes forward.
Let go of yourself and let me through.
Give me your eyes, mouth, mind,
and heart, moment by moment.

I am you.
 You are me.
  We are one.

The day is blessed
and we are a blessing in it.

Our adventure awaits.

DAY 16

God, what would you have me say and do today?

Be sensitive.
Feel others' pains, challenges, and burdens.
    Forget your own today.
  Be there for those who may need
to be heard and understood.

When you ask others,
   How are you?
ask compassionately, with true concern
for their welfare, happiness, and peace.

Smile with your eyes.

    Allow the gate of
  your willingness
to swing wide open.

Make room in your heart so you may hold
the hurts of those you live and work with.

During casual conversations and chance meetings,
extend a sweet spirit that invites others in.
Then
I will perform a perfect work through you.

A smile, a nod, a loving word, a gentle touch,
a silent attentiveness: your very presence
will be a gift,
  a healing,
    a blessing,
      a miracle.

EVENING REFLECTION

Today's guidance proved a beautiful one. I read it before every planned encounter and was conscious of being more sensitive to others while allowing my own challenges to take a back seat. I found I was able to listen with bigger ears and respond more heartfully. When I asked, *How are you?* I didn't get the usual answer: *Fine.* People responded with more openness and vulnerability. I then felt able to be more helpful, even if that involved simply listening.

People can hear and sense our love and care through our words and our tone of voice. They can see love in our eyes. Our care invites trust and allows others to be more forthcoming.

Today, following the guidance, I was grateful to be helpful in a more conscious way.

How did the guidance unfold in your day today?

DAY 17

God, what would you have me say and do today?

Make room.
Give space for others to be together
without you.

Today, let go of any need to be needed.
Let your ego take this day off.

Relax.

Be alive without needing, wanting,
or desiring.

Forgive the parts of you that find
this difficult. Embrace them without resistance
or guilt.

This is how you grow.

Doing this will expand your soul
in a beautiful way.
New vistas of spirit will come into view.
Take them in and let them fill you.

If you can do this, you will feel more able to love
unconditionally.

Make room.
        Give space today.

DAY 18

God, how would you have me be in the world today?

Be like a soft breeze.
    Caress others with your words.
Surround them with gentle, kind actions –
nothing harsh or sudden.

Imagine you are refreshment for
the soul.
You don't need to do much.
Placing the tiniest bit of beauty into your
interactions
is enough.

Be easy to be around –
lightly felt, gently present –
so that others want to lean into
    your peace, your calm,
your soothing spirit.
Taking in a deep breath of you,
    others receive
        life.

DAY 19

God, what would you have me say and do today?

Laugh.
　　Speak in light tones.
Do not be so serious.
　　Not today.

Play with me.
　　What game?
Hide and seek.
　　Find me in all my hidden places.
　　　　Seek me everywhere;
　　see me hiding in plain sight.
And laugh with me.

Today, life is fun,
　　and so are you.
Breathe
　　deeply and easily.
Let heaviness go.

Today,
　　let the lightness of your being
　　　　shine with joy for all to see.

Will you do this today?

EVENING REFLECTION

I was not in a laughing mood today. This guidance was especially challenging and I forgot to carry it with me on my morning errands, which included visits to my accountant, the car mechanic, and an office supply store.

Laugh? Hardly.

After I got home and collected my guidance, I ventured to the post office. The post office and laughing don't traditionally go together, but I found myself finding places in conversation where I could infuse some humour and make the interaction lighter and more jovial.

And it worked. I made people laugh. Well, some. When we can bring lightness of being to a post office, a copy place, and a car mechanic, we are doing good work in the world!

While eating dinner, a family member read from a paper on Hamlet. "Hamlet lost his ability to laugh. He lost his mirth and doesn't know why." This coincidence affirmed that the message of laughing had been a perfect one for the day.

How did you do?

DAY 20

God, what would you have me say and do today?

Treat others
the way you would like to be treated.

Live into this today.

Extend it from moment to moment.
Let it inform each encounter.
Imagine that everything you say to others
is being said to you.
Speak not from the standpoint of your
problems, worries, and fears,
but from your love, hope, and faith.

Imagine that all you do to others is also done
to you.
Be guided not by your ego, agenda, or ambitions
but by your care for the joy
and well-being of others.

You will deepen the well of compassion
you draw from,
increase the sensitivity of your soul,
and expand your spirit in new ways.

What a gift to give yourself today.

Do you want it?

EVENING REFLECTION

Well, I tried.

I am amazed at how the daily guidance seems to bring up the very things that test me. It was hard work to keep my ego from being the one in charge today. I really had to tell my ego that it wasn't the boss of me. I kept putting myself in the other person's shoes as best I could, so that the other was not *other*, but same. This work did make me more aware of how I treat others.

When we do extend ourselves in this way, we can make a beachhead in another person's soul and see him or her as even more than brother or sister. We can see others as ourselves. We can also become aware of how we speak to ourselves, and how we would like others to treat us.

Today's message has ongoing usefulness for me. How did you do with it?

DAY 21

God, how would you have me be in the world today?

Be like a fragrant flower
that knows its own beauty
   without claiming it as its own.

Be seen...but be unobtrusive.

Walk softly.
   Bend gently in the breeze.

Share your sweetness easily;
let it flow from you without effort.

Be kind and forgiving.
   Remember
      that you are firmly rooted in me.

   Let the light of day open your heart,
  and may your presence
bless everyone today.

EVENING REFLECTION

It did not take long before I was tested on this guidance. About the same time as I finished writing this, my 12-year-old son came and stood at my office door. It was 6:30 a.m. and there he was with headphones on and the latest mini music player in hand. He on one side of the door, planted firmly in the world of technology and constant stimulation, bouncing to the beat, and I on the other, in silence, resting in the glow of communing with God.

We looked at each other. Okay, we stared. I wondered what he was looking at. It was a sort of diffuse look, as if he were staring past me. I thought perhaps he was seeing the heavenly light surrounding me. (Okay, that was my ego talking.) Or more likely, he was wondering if it was okay to enter my space. I wasn't quite ready for human contact, and was thinking *No* as he came in.

He walked up to me and said in a bright, innocent tone, "Good morning."

"Darn," I thought. He was just a fragrant flower ... *without* a morning meditation. And he had beaten me at my own game. He got there first! How humbling. I did, however, regroup – and chimed back, "Good morning." And he bounced away joyfully.

Let's just say that what my son gave me was – a wake-up call.

How long was it before your first test?

DAY 22

God, how would you have me be in the world today?

Be open.
Be receptive to ideas not your own.

Listen for, and hear with your heart,
my inner *Yes*.

As I have given ideas, thoughts, and leanings
to you, I have also given them to all others.

Be joyful for your gifts, and just as joyful
for the gifts that others have.
   They are all gifts of mine.

Be welcoming and inviting.
   Be grateful you
      do not hold all things.
If you did, would you learn to share?

Expect all things to work together for good.
Breathe easily and watch how
   I unfold the journey.
Be at peace with your life today.

Trust.
   Listen.
      Stay open.
         Relax.
            Laugh.

Enjoy me in all.
   Enjoy me in all.

EVENING REFLECTION

I attended a meeting where project ideas were offered for future consideration. I had previously put forth an idea that I thought was good. But today an idea that was amazingly creative and brilliant came from another person. I loved the vision offered and hesitated in my applause only for a moment (ah, ego). However, I did jokingly comment, "God likes you better than me," which I instantly recognized as my ego invoking envy. However, the part of me that was aware of my ego's game won out.

I was thankful that God had blessed this artist with his unique mind. And I felt grateful to be working with such a creative group of people.

How did today's guidance speak to your day?

DAY 23

God, what would you have me say and do today?

Be gentle with yourself.

Accepting your humanity
is deeply important.

Forgive yourself whenever
anger, jealousy, or shame come up.
These are your unhealed wounds, whatever
the size.

Breathe and let compassion fill you.
    Then extend this compassion
        toward any person or situation
            that disturbs your peace.

Remember that you are divine.
You are made of love in order to love.

Do not shrink or recoil.
    Understand human nature.

Ask for whatever you need.
    Believe in my love for you.
        Breathe it in – and pass it on.
    Love all today.

Love.

DAY 24

God, what would you have me say and do today?

Speak in a manner that honours those you meet.
Be sincere in your acknowledgments.
Move in love.
Fill your gaze
with appreciation for those whose paths you
cross,
for they are divine beings.

Walk amongst saints today –
    and include yourself as one.

Hold deep gratitude
for those with whom you are sharing
your life journey.

Have no need to achieve notice for yourself,
but raise the esteem of those you speak with
by focusing on them with your full attention
and care.

Be vigilant.
Watch for anything
that hinders the giving of unconditional love
and high regard.

Overcome your blocks with joy for life
and respect for all.

Today, all is divine,
    all is miracle,
        all is love.

EVENING REFLECTION

Even as I become familiar with the synchronicity of the guidance and the challenges of each day, I am still constantly amazed. It is ever so clear that the wisdom and guidance of God are always available when we open ourselves to them. And you open yourself to wisdom and guidance by asking for them. Then you allow yourself to receive. How? By paying attention to your thoughts, your feelings, your intuition, and your gut.

Today was poignant. We had a family reunion of sorts. I was in Atlanta to see my mother, who had cooked a wonderful dinner of traditional soul food and invited the extended family over. The conversations were joyous, and the family closeness was precious. We prayed, sang, ate, talked, and laughed together and enjoyed each other immensely.

I stayed aware of the guidance and it helped me to focus on each person I talked with. I looked upon each person with appreciation and took special care to make sure the shy ones knew they were heard and appreciated. I listened eagerly and gently touched a shoulder or patted a back to affirm presence. I saw each person as a miracle: each child, teenager, young adult, middle-ager, and senior. I do not know how my behaviour registered with them, but the guidance ushered me into a rich, awakened experience of appreciation and gratitude for the people close to me.

Today was sweet – and the guidance, divine.

How did you do with this today?

DAY 25

God, what would you have me say and do today?

Rest in peace.
    Do not be anxious.
Stay calm, no matter what transpires.

Speak slowly;
    breathe deeply.
Do this intentionally,
especially when you feel
tension or worry arise.

Remember past successes.
    Remember that I am
aware of all you go through
and am working on your behalf.

Trust the unfolding of the day,
    and maintain a peacefulness
that allows you to relax
while I work in and through you.

As the day unfolds
    be thankful for your life –
even for the challenges and problems you face.
I use all for your spiritual benefit.

Act with grace today.
    Have faith that all is well.
Breathe deeply.
Stay calm.

Witness the unfolding of my providence.

Rest...in peace.

DAY 26

God, what would you have me say and do today?

Be refreshing,
like a cleansing rain.
   Let words that awaken joy
and water the heart with love
fall from your mouth.

Let the sound of your voice be wet
with laughter, and may it splash
blessing onto everyone you speak with.

Say what is true and helpful.

Be clear in your actions,
that others may see your best intentions.

May you comfort those in need,
sharing the water of tears, if need be,
as you become one with their pain.

May you flow where I lead today.
Stay aware of
wisdom and grace
pouring out as you meet
each circumstance and opportunity.

Be refreshing.
Be joy alive.
Wash away negativity with appreciation and
gratitude.
Live with a clean heart.
Be the living water of life today.
Refresh
      and be refreshed.

Today was relatively easy upon first thought, because I didn't see many people. But on further reflection, I realized it had not been so simple. The people I had engaged with needed specific kinds of responses and energy.

First, I met an old high school friend for lunch, and we caught up on years of life. Then my sister came by with a colleague from overseas she wanted me to meet. We all conversed for a few hours, which included having dinner together. At the end of the day I sat with my ageing mother as we talked and watched one of her favorite television shows.

Each encounter was beautiful and drew upon my energy differently. My high school friend needed patient ears to listen to him as he retraced life events and their accumulated meaning. My sister's friend received a phone call during his visit telling of the death of an acquaintance. I sat quietly across from him while he offered condolences and prayer. After the call, he shared the situation back home. I empathized deeply as his sadness poured out. So I lived the part of the guidance about comforting someone today. I needed to be patient and attentive to my mother's health needs even as we sat enjoying television. We laughed and simply appreciated sitting together.

I hope I was able to refresh today as the first sentence of the guidance encourages. But if not, rain fell most of the day, and I am sure it did refresh things.

Divinity always has a backup plan.

DAY 27

God, how would you have me be in the world today?

Be a jewel.
    Be beautiful in all you do and say.
Be of great value, and offer value
in all interactions.

Dazzle! Sparkle! Shine!

    Hold light within the core of
your being
    so that your beauty and love
shine from the inside out.

Remember the divine ground from which you
    come, and remember that it
    has given you the
qualities you possess.
Use them with grace, appreciation, and humility.
Use them with power, confidence, and purpose.

Yes...
be a jewel in the world today.

Glimmer
    with my holy
        and sacred brilliance,
    and add beauty wherever you are.

Yes...
be a precious gem today.

Dazzle! Sparkle! Shine!

Today my sister recruited me to work with a high school senior on an essay and research project. The student needed to complete the project in order to graduate. It was a somewhat stressful situation because the student was way behind in his work, through no fault of his own.

In steps my sister.

I happened to be in town visiting our mother and was called upon to help out. I drove an hour to meet with the student, who happened to share my first and last initials. We also shared an interest in the arts, as he wanted to become a professional actor.

The pressure of having to write a long paper rather quickly was palpable. The guidance reminded me that I needed to act as mentor and point of inspiration for the young man. As we got to the nitty-gritty of the research paper, the pressure mounted; I stayed conscious of the guidance and each part came into play when needed.

The student and I completed our task, had fun, and connected in a deep and meaningful way. I drove home knowing that I had lived out this guidance in one fell swoop with one human being.

What was your experience with today's guidance?

DAY 28

God, what would you have me say and do today?

Be watchful...
   Be helpful.
Speak with patience and understanding.

Take no offence
but be like water
and adapt to the shape of the day.

Know that you are loved,
   and walk in that knowledge.

Be a soft cushion for others to rest on.

May your love be deep and strong today.
May your emotions remain peaceful today.
May you look upon the day with thankfulness.

   Be joyful all day
and watch the divine play unfold!

EVENING REFLECTION

To adapt to the shape of the day was a beautiful guidance to live into. It took the pressure off, and I found myself just letting things be without feeling the need to control. I offered my ideas in meetings without a sense of ownership. I found I spoke easily and waited for a response with much less ego involvement and defensiveness in my inner stance than usual.

The fun in it all is that I am aware that I am doing this. I can feel the difference between doing it and not. The goal is to become more and more able to follow the guidance without thinking about it. However, it is a wonderful gift to have help along the way.

The guidance's reminder that I am loved also allowed a relaxation within my being that made the day flow without my needing or desiring anything from anyone. What an experience!

Be a soft cushion for others to rest on – this was the most surprising item of the guidance. During my encounters with others throughout the day, I loved the feeling of being a soft cushion for them to rest upon. I seemed to move my body more smoothly and take things in stride; I didn't feel as though I had to comment on this or that. I listened in a loving and accepting way and let the words of others sink in.

Watching – just watching – allowed me to enjoy and appreciate the gifts, personalities, and even the moods and dispositions of those I shared life with today. Today's guidance grew on me as I sank deeper and deeper into its wisdom. I think I grew into it also.

How did you live this one?

DAY 29

God, what would you have me say and do today?

Be like a mountain standing in the blue sky.

Make love a strength in your being today.
Stand up for those you love; for those who need
your strength and support.

With your words, give others beauty and light,
warmth and comfort.

Today you are strong enough to protect
others' needs. Do not think about yourself.

Let your resolve stand you above the goings-on
of the day.

Rise into divinity when you feel yourself
becoming self-centred or needy.

Maintain your high resolve to stay in the light;
remain in the sunshine of love, grace, care, and
compassion.

Breathe in fresh air,
and bask in the breezes of love, understanding,
patience, gentleness, and goodness.

Stand with and look out for those
you come in contact with today:
    those you love,
        and those you do not know.

Root yourself in the ground of divinity
and gain the resources to live into this today.

Should this guidance become difficult,
don't give up.
        Rise up.

Will you do this today?

EVENING REFLECTION

It did not take more than half an hour for me to be
tested in this guidance.

I was presented with a personal challenge that took a
tremendous amount of inner fortitude, love, and
strength to meet. I did not see it coming. Have you
ever been faced with a powerful challenge you didn't
ask for or see coming?

Spiritual guidance happens in many ways: perhaps as
a response to prayer, or as words of wisdom that we
recognize as a message for us. The point is that when
Spirit guides us to act or speak a certain way, even
when we do not know why, it is wise to follow the
lead of God's holy spirit. It is not blind obedience
that I am talking about. It is trust – trust in God's
guidance based on our own past experiences of divine
guidance, regardless of whether the results were what
we wanted. Divine trust means knowing that there is
a bigger picture, one which we may not see or even be
privy to. Thus the great spiritual challenge: *Let go
and let God.*

When we let go and let God, we become servants of
the Divine, which then allows us to become angels for
others at any time.

DAY 30

God, how would you have me be in the world today?

Be like a blossom in springtime,
   waking to a new beginning:
opening, growing,
fresh, alive,
and glad to be so.

Be fragrant in what you say and do.
Leave a sweet scent wherever you go.

Let your attitudes and responses
be beautiful to behold.

Draw spiritual nourishment from the deep
and ever-flowing source
of replenishment and renewal.

Always lean toward the light of divinity.
Let its warm and peaceful rays of wisdom
and loving guidance surround you
as you journey through the day.

Speak with the beauty of your whole being
and allow others to look upon you
while you stand in my glow, grace, and serenity.

Keep blossoming today;
allow new aspects of your beauty to unfold
through your face, mannerisms, and temperament.

Enjoy being beautiful today...
   all day.

DAY 31

God, what would you have me say and do today?

Say what is uplifting.
   Do what is life-building.

   Speak from the centre of your soul,
not from the mind;
   from the depths of your being,
not the surface.
   Let words and actions flow from your heart,
      the loving core of your existence.

   Move with a peaceful grace,
   with slower, surer movements that
exude blessing and divinity.

This energy and focus will allow you to
   to move through the day
      as the divine being you are –
         as an angel on earth.

   Let love overflow the banks of your being
   and spill blessings on all.

How wonderful is that?

EVENING REFLECTION

Today was relatively easy – that is, until 5:30 p.m. or so when I had a visit from a loved one who is moving through loss, grief, and soul disorientation.

It can be difficult to speak peacefully to someone in great pain. Peace can feel disturbing to someone who is not in it themselves. Speaking peacefully can provoke an attack from the other, one that is difficult to defend against, no matter what we say and even if we agree with all the other is saying! They want to fight God, the world, and most things in it. Silence does not win us anything either, except charges of insensitivity and not caring. We are a complicated species.

This guidance, however, helped me stay calmer than I may have been otherwise. I moved a little more slowly than usual and spoke with quiet assurance of positive things to come. I delivered such hope in an uplifting manner and tone of voice. But if another person does not want for themselves even the possibility of peace then there is not much we can do, except pray.

Peace is ultimately between each of us and God. This guidance helped me to stay connected to the resources of peace in the midst of its opposite.

How did you do today?

God, what would you have me say and do today?

Do not speak hastily.
Listen deeply
and respond with genuine heart.

Feel what is in your soul. Look within
and be with your truth.

Rest inside yourself
and enjoy who you are.

Watch for things that may surprise you
and then investigate them.

See where you have grown.
Notice the boundaries of your own maturity.

Look around.
Imagine where you are going.

Be thankful for the paths you have travelled
and sense your spirit's excitement
for the soul journey to come.

Today is a day of introspection.
Look inward with wonder
and awe.

DAY 33

God, what would you have me say and do today?

Remember the child in you.

Honour the vulnerable aspects of your being.
Love gently your fears, pains, and wonderings.

Adopt this precious part of you. Hold it
with tenderness and compassion,
and bring it into your
protection and understanding.

This child is a gift to you,
and you are a gift to it.
Give this part of you a home
within your higher consciousness.

Hold close to your heart this younger self.
Wrap your arms around...you.

Allow the child that lives and lingers within
to feel your spiritual strength –
to feel the part of you that is sure of me.
Let it feel the part of you that has
unflinching faith,
the part that knows the power of love and light,
the parts that have experienced healing, blessing,
and the negation of fear.

Let the child see through your eyes
    and become like you –
        whole, fearless,
a divine light being.

Today wasn't about how to treat or be with other people or how to be in the world. It was about recognizing and acknowledging the part of me that is still a child and then giving it the attention and TLC it needs.

A recurring dream about being asked to adopt a homeless, abandoned child, one who had my initials and who looked somewhat like me, made it clear that I was being guided to integrate the part of me – the child in me – that had been left on his own.

This precious guidance led me to recognize, honour, and begin to consciously integrate a childhood trauma. I remember the intense fear I experienced when I was six years old, and I want to say to that young guy, "Hello, little David. You are now home. You are protected, loved, and out of danger. Be not afraid any longer."

How was your experience of being asked to remember the child in you?

DAY 34

God, what would you have me say and do today?

Be gentle and sensitive.
    Make no effort to push for anything.
Let things flow; take things in stride.

Today, relax as you choose what to do.
    Speak with love.
Let others know that you appreciate them.

Be present for others while giving them space.

Be open to a new, subtler level of sensitivity
    to the states of mind and being of others.

Be understanding and have no judgment;
    say what is loving and supportive.

This is a day of gentle being for you.
    Let natural grace flow from you.

This will be your gift today...
    graceful conversation and ease of interaction.

Don't fake anything.
    No pretense of any kind today.

Be strong in your resolve to do this.
Let nothing get in your way.

EVENING REFLECTION

Today was quite a success – until about 9:00 p.m.

An issue surfaced at a gathering that I tried to remain quiet about because I had strong opinions that I believed were not useful in that context. I don't have a very good poker face though, and someone asked me what was wrong. When I had my say, my words were met with anger. Even though I was coming from a place of love and care, my opinion was received in a way I had not intended.

Had I been gentle and sensitive when I finally spoke? I thought I had been.

Did I speak lovingly? Yes. (I thought I did, anyway.)

Was I judgmental? Yes, I had some judgment, even though what I said was loving and supportive.

Did I let something get in the way? Yes – me!

Uuggh!

I almost made it. Sometimes the real test happens at the end of the day!

Watch out for 9:00 p.m!

DAY 35

God, how would you have me be in the world today?

Be welcoming and open,
like the meadows and plains.

Hold on to nothing, and meet all
without judgment or opinion.

Be a container for others to inhabit.
Let them hear and see themselves
through your clear and open spirit.

Invite with your eyes, heart, and speech.

Be a resting place for the sojourners
you meet today.

Refresh with your encouragement,
purify with your hope,
nourish with your trust,
strengthen with your faith.

Let the borders of your being extend outward;
make a safe place for others
to roam, rest, and replenish.

All are welcome. All are welcome.

EVENING REFLECTION

At 4:00 p.m., an old friend came to visit. He was going through a rough life change and needed a warm welcome. I had not seen this person in a few years and was glad to listen, share a meal, and learn the details of his journey.

As the friend was preparing to leave, to my surprise he acknowledged my hospitality and acceptance. Furthermore, he said, "I think this is the beginning of a turnaround for me."

I was glad to hear that, and while I take no credit for it, perhaps being conscious of the guidance to be an open, welcoming spirit contributed to his positive change.

We all need assisted living at certain times. Sometimes the assistance comes in the form of someone listening to us and responding with faith or a positive outlook.

DAY 36

God, what would you have me say and do today?

Today, think thoughts that are positive,
    good and loving.
    Do not allow negativity to win over
      your mind, emotions, or attitude.

It is not necessary to speak much.
    Just think with a heart of love,
      and allow those thoughts
    to guide your speech
and actions.

No great effort is necessary –
    perhaps just gentle redirection when needed.

Be patient today.
    Let me work things out while you watch,
      while you think with divine intention,
        while you stay in touch with me.

      Be calm and peaceful today,
      even in moments of excitement
    and busyness.

Breathe in deeply
and let the goodness of life fill you.

Think, speak, and act from a place of
    freshness, blessing, and the joy of being...
      of being
        alive.

EVENING REFLECTION

This proved to be a really beautiful guidance today, particularly the *not necessary to speak much* part. It allowed me to connect to the day in a unique manner. My silence made me more aware of my senses.

I noticed that not speaking allowed patience to be a stronger quality in my interactions. I was more aware of my thinking; I was even able to stop the gushing fountain of automatic thinking. I could then tell my brain what to think. In other words, I could think for myself instead of letting my brain think for me. Then I injected positive thought.

Where I would have spoken reflexively, I sometimes simply smiled or touched the other person on the shoulder instead, which proved to be a stronger communication than my words would have been. At other times, I gave a look filled with joy and appreciation. They got it, and I didn't have to say a word.

Being calm and peaceful in the midst of busyness is akin to being the eye of the storm. What a great feeling! We can all do this in every area of life. Practice breathing in the goodness of life without judging or labelling – without speaking much at all. Just absorb it, and then offer it from your heart.

DAY 37

God, what would you have me say and do today?

Be like the banks of a river.
Hold with love all those
you encounter
but let them flow
as they will.
Say and do that which supports
and allows their ease of movement.

See them as they walk, talk,
and find their way through the day.
You are to hold the day in watchful
allowance and appreciation,
letting others use your
strength and grounding...
holding all that occurs with
your gentle smile
and a softness
that says,
all is well.
Yes,
be like the banks of a river.

EVENING REFLECTION

Focusing my attention on holding space for people as they lived the day became a profound privilege. Of course, no one knew I was envisioning myself as a riverbank, but holding this vision evoked a profound awareness that each life is precious and has an individual path. It called for me to give space and stay out of the way while remaining involved. The banks of a river provide guidelines for the water's journey. Of course, the water – and people – can overflow the boundaries altogether. As I lived into this powerful vision, I sensed that the guidance was not about trying to control anything or anyone, but about being a resource, and then only if invited.

This evening I attended a high school *a cappella* singing competition. As the young people waited their turns to perform, I could sense their nervousness and excitement. I imagined surrounding them all with supportive energy. I do not know if anyone felt it, but it did make me smile, nod my head, and applaud with joy and perhaps more emphasis and overtness than I might have shown otherwise.

This creative visualization proved to be a powerful and enjoyable tool with which to connect with others in a positive, supportive manner.

What was your experience with the guidance today?

DAY 38

God, what would you have me say and do today?

Today,
    be thankful.
        Give thanks for all things.

This simple task has within it great power.
    The benefits for you
        and the world are tremendous.

So today, for everyone you see,
    give thanks.
For all things said to you –
both the kind and the unwanted –
    be thankful,
knowing that I work all things
    for your benefit.

Be like the sun rising on a clear morning.
    Give warmth and light.
Offer reassurance of my presence,
    my love,
        my life-giving sustenance,
          and my power,
through which all things are made possible.

Today, be in awe of life itself.
    Let the wonder of it envelop you.

Give thanks for life
    and the beauty of it
        and in it.

Give thanks for all things today.
    For all things.

    Will you do this?

EVENING REFLECTION

The synchronicity of the daily guidance and the challenges encountered while living into it amazes me every time. Today was a beautiful day. I went to a gathering of people I had not seen in many years. The group included people who knew of me before I was born, as they were friends of my parents when I was in the womb. I took a loved one with me and had a very enjoyable time.

On the way home, a simple comment led to a heated discussion that brought up some past wounds. I had enough awareness to be able to withdraw from conflict and try to quell the storm, but peace was difficult to come by. Remembering the day's guidance, I found the strength to offer that I was thankful for the issues brought forth – but we spent the remaining drive-time in silence, for which I was also thankful.

Eventually the storm passed and we were able to speak our truths more peacefully and move on. But it took the storm to clear the air. At the time it was not an easy thing to deal with, but I am thankful that all things are contained in the love and grace of Divinity.

How did you fare?

DAY 39

God, what would you have me say and do today?

Be forgiving today.

Allow yourself and everyone you encounter
to be human, with all the frailties
and shortcomings that are part of being human.

Be gentle and compassionate with your failings,
and understand those of others.
Know all are doing their best
in any moment.

Remembering that all things are done
out of love or as cries for love,
find it within yourself to be a soft place of love.
Let go of hurts and past wrongs
done to you or by you.

Today offers an opportunity to grow.
Each act of forgiveness – of letting go –
is a step along the path
of your continuing spiritual growth.

Each failure is a lesson
from which to grow.
So, be gentle.
All are learning.

Today, let the things that happened yesterday,
or years ago, be where they belong –
in the past.

Claim a new beginning in this new day.
Remember that being human is not easy.
Be gentle with yourself.

Breathe deeply. Breathe easily. Let go. Forgive.
Live in the light and freedom
   of unconditional love today.

EVENING REFLECTION

I am writing this reflection at 9:45 a.m. I wrote the guidance at 7:30 a.m. Already I have been both tested and affirmed. It seems that I must live into what I write with haste and without delay! There is no warm-up period or waiting until I leave the house.

Even as I have spent hours, days, and years writing a daily guidance (or better, having it write me), my offer to God that I want to be an instrument of divinity still comes with the concomitant silent question, *How can I know that my daily writings are a creation of Spirit*? One way I receive an answer is through the synchronicity I experience when the test specifically targets a day's guidance.

This morning, as I was reading the last chapter of a wonderful inspirational book, I came across several paragraphs that essentially stated the same thing I had just written in the guidance. And they were written using almost the same words! That kind of tight synchronicity always surprises me, mostly because I don't see it coming. The experience is beautiful, and deeply affirming of the reality and presence of God in my personal life. It reassures me of Divinity's grace and ability to guide, and it strengthens my inner knowing that there is no space between me and the Divine One. It is an experience of being seen and cared for. I know that God knows who I am and where I am. Furthermore, it is personal proof that Divinity is alive and conscious and can wink at me in joy, celebration, and partnership during my spiritual journey.

No matter what else happens today, I have already had an extraordinary moment with Divinity. I hope you have your own divine moment today.

DAY 40

God, what would you have me say and do today?

Be like fresh rain.
    Pour softly and gently onto the souls
    you encounter today.

Wet hearts with words that refresh
    and bring love's dew.

Let your actions
    moisten the hardness in others
        as you speak soft words filled with
           love, hope, and trust.

Let divine rain fall into you.
    Keep your heart open to my touch.

Be filled with the gift of love.
    It will keep you moist and supple
    that you may gift others
as you go through the day.

Let the outpouring of your actions
    be a shower of love,
and watch how the garden of love grows.

DAY 41

God, how would you have me be in the world today?

Be a river of peace.
    Let all that flows from you
        be drenched in peace.
Let your words bring calmness and stillness.
    Let your eyes shine with grace.
        Let your manner
    radiate love's gracefulness.
Let respect and appreciation wash over
        those you journey with today.
    Know that all you say and do
    emerges from divinity
and merges back into divinity.
Let the sacred current carry you through the day,
as you bring refreshment to your encounters.

      Walk in peace.
    Speak peace.
Be peace.
    Flow...
      like a river of
        peace.

DAY 42

God, what would you have me say and do today?

Be grounded.
Be solid.

Be solid enough for others to stand on
as you support them with the strength
of love.

Be sturdy enough that others may use
your wisdom and encouragement as a base
from which to lift off
toward distant horizons, dreams, and goals.

Hold all souls with a consistency of being
that welcomes and upholds.
Allow others to feel the strength
of your presence and personhood.

To do this, you must be grounded in me.
You must stay rooted in my love for you
and draw upon the ready grace
given to all who ask –
and are ready to receive.

If you do this today,
you will become stronger and wiser.
You will feel the might of your spirit
and you will grow in grace and beauty.

It will be a good day indeed.

EVENING REFLECTION

It takes only one person to challenge me to live a daily guidance (and thus grow from it). I encountered very few people today. However, of the few I did encounter, one in particular proved the guidance.

As I was heading to the gym this afternoon someone contacted me to ask for my help in reviewing an important project he was working on. He was under a deadline and hoped I could make myself available for an hour. As I was not on a tight schedule I realized I could accommodate his request. Plus, it wasn't often this person asked for help. I knew my help would be appreciated, and my time was more flexible than the person's deadline.

Even though I changed my plans, I still carried the feeling of wanting to do that workout without delay. I also realized that I was being challenged by the guidance. And, although it would have been fine to keep to my original schedule, I knew I could work it around my friend's request. I also knew that the crux of my *why now* attitude was that the club had a new exercise machine I had sort of fallen in love with and couldn't wait to get back to. I remembered the first line of the guidance, and that (along with knowing that the new machine would still be there) helped to change my budding frustration to calm willingness to let go and let Divinity guide my plans.

And for the next hour I poured over my friend's project. He thanked me generously and told me he had been feeling a little shaky and was glad I could affirm his work.

Thinking of the guidance, I had to laugh about helping someone on shaky ground.

I still got my workout in – and felt stronger and even more solid afterwards.

DAY 43

God, what would you have me say and do today?

Be a poet of the day...
    Be aware, on a grand scale,
    of what you say and do.

From a higher, divine perspective
    see how your actions and reactions
        create a living poem about life today
    that recites in the depths of your being
and echoes throughout all your affairs.

Let your lyric be beauty, love,
    kindness, and generosity.

Be mindful of the stanzas you fashion
    with your movements,
and the feelings you engender
    with your tone of voice.

Be inspired by recognizing
    divine essence in all things.

    Let the magnificence of nature,
    the wonder of creation,
and the uniqueness of every being
sink in and touch your spirit.

Craft your poem
    with grace, compassion, and joy.
        Let it shine in your soul.

Inspire angels.

EVENING REFLECTION

I attended an awards ceremony today at a private school and, as the new face in this small community, met many people I didn't know. I re-read today's guidance just before immersing in the handshakes and polite-isms of the gathering. I was aware of being somewhat self-conscious. But I was also aware of seeing (or at least looking for) divine essence in everyone I met. The awkwardness I felt lessened as I focused more on the presence of divinity.

Later in the day, I attended an evening concert at a local high school. During the performance, several young boys kept kicking my seat and talking. Finally, I turned and said something to them. I don't know how poetically it came out, but I do know that remembering the guidance helped me be as nice as I could be in those irritating moments. They stopped kicking my seat but kept talking. I ended up moving to keep my own peace, which may have been the most poetic stanza of the day!

How did you do?

DAY 44

God, what would you have me say and do today?

Today I would have your awareness
that all is blessed
when placed in my care.

All things, when brought to me, are
seen in the light of my love and compassion –
even war, tragedy, poverty, and hunger.

Every human endeavour, when brought to me,
is seen in its purest
and most innocent essence.

Bring all things to me in prayer, meditation, and
sacred song;
surrender your own mind to the light of my
wisdom.

Insight, revelation, and knowledge are revealed –
some to you, some to others –
even as some mysteries
remain hidden for another day or another time.

Give me your awareness and I will
fill it with light and love.
My gift to you today: you will see with
divine eyes.

EVENING REFLECTION

Sometimes a guidance comes that is more a message of what God might be like or might do. I have learned to be faithful in writing whatever comes through. Whatever it is that lets the guidance come through – whether it is my higher wisdom in conjunction with my academic spiritual training, or a more direct communication from God that bypasses the right brain – it is all God, all divine – for that is my intention when I ask.

In this guidance, I was asked to give my awareness back to God.

The way I see the world is partly influenced by the baggage I carry: baggage life has handed me, or that I have bought into, sometimes unconsciously. Our ego and subconscious hold secrets we may not gain awareness of until we go into therapy or pursue a spiritual path that opens us to insight, understanding, and grace.

Today I was reminded that I can look out upon the world with divine vision and see even the worst of our world through the eyes of love and grace.

DAY 45

God, what would you have me say and do today?

Be quiet.
Be the master of your mind today.
  Do not let it think whatever it wants.

Quiet the loud thoughts
and discern my voice.

Attune your hearing to the vast
inner depths of your being.

Let all occurrences be filtered through this portal.
Sift the day through divine grace.

      Listen with your heart.
      Think with your heart.

Act and speak from the quiet depths
of your soul.
Sound love through your lips.
Receive the day
      with gratitude
as quiet becomes the powerful voice of your
being.

DAY 46

God, what would you have me say and do today?

Be a soft breeze.
      Speak gently,
and move without hurry.
Take your time.
Caress the day and all it holds
      with the lightness of your being.
Even the weightiest conversations
and challenges can be met with this
      lightness
when you remember I am holding it all.

      Breathe in with appreciation.
Resolve to stay even-keeled
and mellow, no matter the chaos
      around you
        or in you.

For today, leave it with me.

Look out on the world
   through eyes of love
and heart of kindness.

Speak and act from this posture.
      Are you willing to do this today?

DAY 47

God, what would you have me say and do today?

Be kind to yourself.
You are doing the best you can.

Have compassion for your own troubles.
Be patient, and know that
 I am in the midst of them
with love and light on your behalf.

Do not get ruffled when unexpected events
challenge your peace.
Remember you are already greatly blessed.
Facing challenges can help you grow
into a more beautiful creation.

 Love your life.

Stay joyful; bear everything with humility.
Ups and downs come
 like waves in the sea and
 I move in them all,
working all things for good.
So be patient, loving, and kind
as my divine work unfolds.

EVENING REFLECTION

This was another example of a guidance becoming more meaningful and powerful as the day wore on.

Today I encountered unexpected expenses. My daughter's car windows became inoperative – they were down, and it was raining! I also received a bill for an unexpected hike in her college tuition. Then there came a new car insurance bill. Throw in a couple more unexpected financial costs (appliance repairs) that suddenly came knocking and you get the general downpour of my day.

Of course, these aren't earthshaking events, but they are part of the daily adventure through life's little troubles. Navigating these choppy waves took me out of my natural rhythm, so I followed the first line of the guidance and was kind to myself. For me, it meant taking a deep breath and realizing that I could get back to my work in due course. It also meant being grateful for the means to attend to these things.

Later, I decided to cook a special dinner for my wife and me. Chicken curry, anyone?

And most importantly, in the midst of it all, I reminded myself that I do love my life.

DAY 48

God, what would you have me say and do today?

Be as gentle as you can today;
be as gentle as your humanity will allow.
  And then, go further –
      be even more gentle.

Your strength will remain.
In fact, it takes great inner strength to be gentle.

In this you will surely be tested.
Remember that spiritual progress
demands that your ego be let go.
Use fierce love –
a love committed to love –
to burn through the layers of hardness.

Summon the great strength that I have
  already placed within you

      You can do it.
    Have no doubts.
It may even be somewhat amusing and fun,
if you stay awake to the tricks of your ego
and do not let it
      Edge **G**od **O**ut.

    Be gentle...
  Be gentle...
Be gentle.

DAY 49

God, what would you have me say and do today?

Be content.
Be content about where you are in your life.

Rest in knowing you are exactly where you are
supposed to be.
The divine unfolding never makes an error.

I am love, and love's intent fills all creation.
Your "mistakes" appear simply as life lessons
when viewed from love's vantage point.

You are guided by a power that loves
you with more love than you can hold
within your human frame.

The unfairness of life
tests love and loving.
But even death and suffering are not
out of the purview of my love and care.

      Who you are is my gift to you.
      Who you become is your gift to me.

Be.
Be content today.
  Rest in who you are,
        (*your name here*) of God.

DAY 50

God, what would you have me say and do today?

Be patient, kind, and loving.

Acknowledge where you find this challenging.
Then gather strength of spirit,
     will of mind,
   and resolve of soul,
and push into the love
that you are to share.

Take no offence today.
   Just offer love and kindness.

Pour out kindness and
let love flow into all you do and say.
Let patience sit within you
   like the still water of a calm lake.

Do not be deterred today.
Hold on. It is worth the effort.

          You'll see.

Oh, one more thing...
     Virtue is its own reward.
          You'll see.

DAY 51

God, what would you have me say, or do, or be like today?

Forgive yourself.

     Relax into your humanity.
     Relax and keep on relaxing.
     Allow tension to be released.

Breathe calmly and let all striving rest, even while
working diligently.
     Connect with whatever is enjoyable.

Let your divine nature come through as you
hold back judgment, jealousy, or negativity.

     Feel your own holiness.
     Accept your life as a gift.
     Just be, without any goal or angst.

     Relax and rest in me
     as you accept things as they are now,
     as you accept what was then.

If there is unhappiness, don't disturb it;
connect with your place of joy today.

It need not be demonstrated.
Just recognize joy and let it
          roam through you freely,
          even when confronted by pain
          or challenging emotions.

Claim the freedom found in forgiveness
and the power discovered in joy.

Forgive and be joyous.
Let go and allow your divine
inner light to shine.

Relax.
It's all okay.

DAY 52

God, what would you have me say and do today?

Be open and receptive.

Allow yourself to meet and greet new ideas.
Keep open the door to inspiration and learning.

Hold your wisdom and knowledge lightly
but with appreciation, and allow new
wisdom and insight to be revealed.

Be confident in your path. Know that you offer
much through your personality, character,
accumulated knowledge and understanding.

Listen for guidance.

Be ready to offer your creativity and passion.

Today, let life come to you.
Meet it with joy and optimism.

Remember that divine work is being done
through you and others.
Watch with humble appreciation and gratitude
as the day unfolds.

DAY 53

God, what would you have me say, do, or be like today?

Follow the guidance of your heart today.
Trust its leanings, desires, and motivations.

Be your true self.

Listen to yourself and see where it leads you –
where you lead you.

Speak sincerely from your heart.
Take your time and say what you mean.

Let all you do today be honest.
Do nothing falsely.

Watch with your whole being.
Watch yourself.
Be true to yourself.
Pay attention to yourself and see who you are
– who you really are –
and marvel.

DAY 54

God, what would you have me say and do today?

Be ready.
You will cross a threshold today.
   Something new will come to you,
or be pulled from you,
or call to you from deep inside.
Inspiration is poised to meet
your skills, talents, and desires.
Opportunity is ready to knock.
Be ready.

Keep your senses open and your mind sharp.
Be attentive to your intuition.
   Let creation sing in your soul
      and the universe move in your spirit.

Be flexible
   and
      be ready.

Be ready to recognize the moment of grace
when earth and heaven meet in you
to exchange gifts:
     your gifts to me,
     and my gifts to you.

In this is love shared and genius born.

Be ready.

EVENING REFLECTION

It was surprising to get the words, *be ready*. It took a few minutes after that for the next sentences. It was as if I had to...be ready for it. The rest came in a smooth, steady flow.

Today my wife and I began a process of figuring out how we are going to write songs together. We talked at length about the songwriting parts of our lives and listed the processes we have used to create music.

We decided to create a song about two courting doves that have been gracing our home, and to relate their courtship and togetherness to human life in some way. We didn't know how to begin, but then we had a breakthrough that surprised both of us. As we listened to the cooing sounds of the doves, we began creating the song based on the notes we were hearing.

It was a sweet moment. Our different styles and diverse histories found common ground. We then broke ground and built a new song because we were – ready.

What happened in your day? Were you ready?

DAY 55

God, what would you have me say, do, or be like today?

Keep it simple.
See simplicity in all things today:
      conversations, interactions, reactions.
Even the most complex thing has a
      basic simplicity.
To get to this is to get to peace.

Use simple uncomplicated words.
Be clear and easy to understand.

Keep your face relaxed and your emotions
connected to love, peace, and joy.
      Breathe deeply.

Fear and love are the two
most powerful emotions;
      always choose love.

    Stay out of complex drama today.
    Exude the simple joy of being alive today.
You may choose chaos, complexity, and drama
      tomorrow if you wish.

Today, keep it simple.
See, smile, breathe, love.

EVENING REFLECTION

9:00 a.m.!

It's not evening, but I had to write this.

Just as I finished writing this guidance at 9:00 a.m. I received a text message from my wife. I was waiting for her to get home so that we could go golfing for the first time in a long while and thought she was texting to say she was on her way. I was excited.

But it turned out she was at the flower store. To be fair, she had been up for four hours already, as she had taken a 6:00 a.m. aerobics class – while I slept. So she was actually waiting for me! Even though I was anxious to get going, I texted back, "I can't wait to see the beautiful new additions to our home."

Simple. Loving. Joyful. Peaceful. At least I got it right in that moment.

I breathed deeply and was happy to wait. Besides, the complexities of golf would still be there, even as that course would become a new challenge to keep it simple.

DAY 56

God, what would you have me say, do, or be like today?

Today, gather yourself.
Take stock of your accomplishments.

Breathe deeply.
    Nod your head
with thankfulness
for all you give and receive,
for all you teach and learn,
for all those you love and are loved by.

Know it has all been worked out perfectly.
You are where you are supposed to be.

Breathe into that truth.
    Relax and be okay with it.

Now, sense what is calling you,
pulling you:
        a pursuit, a task, a mission,
            or something undone.

Even in the midst of your busy life,
hear what is calling from deep within and
        gather yourself.
            Your destiny calls you.
                It sounds in your soul.
Turn and move toward it.
Keep moving in its direction. It yearns for you,
and you for it.

Today may be the first day
of another phase of the great adventure called
you!

Breathe,
        and gather yourself.

Today I did what the guidance asked or guided me to do. I sat and pondered, contemplated, and appreciated the things I have done. I then settled into myself – my soul– and felt a lingering feeling of wanting to write and publish some specific works. I could feel a huge *yes* in me as I acknowledged that feeling and committed to moving in its direction.

To gather oneself can take some courage, for gathering calls for introspection, honesty, and coming to terms with things left undone, unsaid, or unconfessed. It is a beautiful process that places you on holy ground alone with God. Gathering is where will, strength, direction, clarity, passion, and purpose come together.

Today I got ready to move. I was affirmed in the projects I am working on, including this book. At this point, I do not know who will publish it, but if you are reading it now, it got published. The writing was an act of faith, a response to the deep calling to create such a book.

How did the day unfold for you? Were you ready?

DAY 57

God, what would you have me say, do, or be like today?

Be fresh air,
   clean spirit,
      and pure soul.

Let your words be life-giving and uplifting.
Let your eyes sparkle with delight.

     What delight?

The delight of being alive,
of being loved and cared for by
me… the one who gave you your life.

Smile with your whole being today.
     How?
By breathing deeply and relaxing,
by being thankful for the gift of your life,
by letting go of tension or anxiety.
Do not force it. Let it happen
in its own way, as it will.

And it will.
     Just breathe deeply, and slowly, and let go.

When you enjoy the lightness of your own being
others will enjoy you
and be refreshed.

A beautiful day awaits…
     Are you ready?

EVENING REFLECTION

I usually carry the guidance in my pocket and read it several times during the day. But I changed pants today and forgot to take the guidance out of my pocket.

I attended an honouring ceremony for students who had finished up a period of gruelling training. The ceremony was small and intimate. I was a new face in this setting and could have easily felt out of place, but I remembered enough of the guidance and focused on being fresh air sparkling with delight. As funny as that may seem, the image was enough to invoke the lightness of my own being, which in turn helped me to not focus on the awkwardness of feeling like an outsider or stranger and thus enjoy the beautiful ceremony.

Once the ceremony ended, I used the images to ease my inner angst. I was able to smile, start conversations, and introduce myself without feeling awkward or uncomfortable.

How did you do with the guidance today?

DAY 58

God, what would you have me do, say, or be like today?

Be the light of the world!

     Consciously emanate the divine within you.
Let it shine out of every pore
     with constancy and sureness.
Remember you are never forsaken.
     It is not possible.

Breathe deeply and glow.

Draw on the power of the universal Christ spirit
     within you.
Transform darkness with a look, a touch,
or a good word as the opportunity presents.
     Intend love in all you do and say.

Fear nothing.
     See beauty.
        Shine.

You are the light of the world.
Enjoy the glow of your own being today.

Shine!

DAY 59

God, what would you have me say, do, or be like, today?

Be relaxed.
     Speak calmly.
Move smoothly.

     Feel the air against your face
as a divine caress.

     Feel the ground beneath you
as the strength of my spirit supporting you
and guiding you forward.

Enjoy all those who cross your path.

     Laugh.
     Be happy to dance with life today.
Let joy tickle you from head to toe.

     All right?

DAY 60

God, what would you have me be like, or say, or do today?

Be aware of your whole being today.
Sense your intimate, expansive, and precious soul.

Feel the life of your life.

Expand your consciousness beyond
the everyday details and take in the reality
of your eternal spirit.

Go about the day's activities immersed in the gift
of just being –
the gift of existence itself.

Take time to connect to the source of life.

Know that you are a gift to creation,
to others, and to yourself,
and know that you are loved beyond measure.

You matter.

Live, speak, and act from this knowing today.

DAY 61

God, what would you have me say, do, or be like today?

Be patient.

Let things develop at a pace that suits
the rhythm of the endeavour.
Relax and watch.
Watch and enjoy.
Let go of the need to make the day's progress
match your own speed.

Allow the pace of faith to govern.
Watch creation's unfolding with joy,
gratitude, and appreciation.
Know that you do not have to do things
by yourself.

There is a higher power.
Feel it flowing through you.
Let it lead and guide.
Float along on its strength, wisdom, and love.

Ride the day
like the child of the universe you are.
Ride the day with awe and wonder.
See amazing things
as you journey.

DAY 62

God, what would you have me be like, or say, or do today?

You are already doing it.
You are open and willing to receive my guidance.

    Stay open today.
Be like dry earth soaking up rain.

Feel the reverberations of my voice as gentle,
rolling thunder in your being.

Let my spirit wash through you
and all your words and actions will be right.

As the desert is replenished by rain, my spirit
will freshen you. Stay open and willing, and seek
my will and the power to live into it moment by
moment.

This is the divine relationship we live, move,
and have our being in:
you and me, together, today.

DAY 63

God, what would you have me say, do, or be like today?

Be a soft cushion.
Allow all things
to rest comfortably with you and in you.

Take things as they come and do not
rush them.
    Let them linger
        or leave as they will.

Work diligently without hurry.
Have calm faith
that all that needs to be accomplished
will be.

Take in the beauty of the day.
    Pause.
Relax and appreciate yourself.

Be grateful for the time you have for your work.

    Pause,
        and breathe deeply.
    Pause,
        and take your time.

Love the day; let it caress you.
Bask in the gift of being.

Find silence and immerse yourself in it,
even if only for a moment or two.

Let quiet hold you softly today,
and be a soft cushion for others.

EVENING REFLECTION

Today's guidance was apropos, as the day was filled with surprises and altered plans. My wife and I were preparing to watch an NBA playoff game on television when we got a frantic call from one of our daughters – she had lost the keys to her car. *Soft cushion time.* My wife quickly opted to deliver the spare keys while I stayed home with our 12-year-old son and his friend who were making loud and joyful noise with their antics. She knew she was getting the better deal here.

Being a soft cushion helped me to stay peaceful and thus helped my daughter stay calm in the midst of one of life's unplanned happenings. I spoke steadily and calmly to her on the phone, confident that things would be well – and already were.

As for spending precious time with my wife, we decided to record the game and view it later. *Soft cushion for us.*

As the lost car key event turned out to be an hours-long adventure, I was alone much of this day. I took the opportunity to follow the guidance further by immersing myself in the silence of my office. I had plenty of opportunity to breathe deeply and feel what might be calling me. I paid bills, organized my desk, and threw away lots of unneeded papers, while enjoying the boys off and on. Then my other daughter called to say she had cancelled her plan to visit us soon. *Soft cushion time again.* I supported her decision while letting her know I would look forward to seeing her the next time she was available. It was my opportunity to practice letting things be what they are without interfering.

Being a soft cushion is a very useful way to be – especially on days like today.

How did you fare?

DAY 64

God, what would you have me say, do, or be like today?

Be grounded.
　　　Be gentle.
　　　　　Be gracious.
Be deeply rooted in your connection
　　to my divine source
　　　　of peace, calm, and wisdom.

Do not let your mind think whatever it wants.
Always speak lovingly and carefully.

Connect with me,
　　then speak,
　　　　move,
　　　　　　act.

You will be
guided moment by moment
when you are connected to the heart
of your being.

Let your emotions rest in my reservoir
of strength and love.
Accept your challenges, knowing they are
in my good care.

Enjoy this day.
　　Show love.
　　　　Be peace.
Let your eyes shine with divine light,
and let your soul rest in deep calm.

DAY 65

God, what would you have me say, do, or be like today?

Today, just be
human.
Simply be,
without trying to stand out in some way.

Make being courteous and kind your agenda.

Notice your thoughts
but don't make too much of them. Just notice them.

Breathe smoothly. Imagine the world
as a deeply loved family member
or an innocent child.

Be gentle with yourself today,
and share that gift of soul
in all you do and say.

Accept the beauty and uniqueness
of your humanity today.

Feel the inner glow of life itself and
look outward to see...
...to see just how amazing being human is.

EVENING REFLECTION

Being conscious of my humanity today was comforting and even freeing. And as complicated as being human is, it was refreshing to live the day stripped down to being courteous, kind, and non-judgmental.

Conscious breathing can, by itself, make me aware of the precious gift of being alive.

Practicing seeing the world as a loved one or as an innocent child was both challenging and beautiful. There arose within me a sense of forgiveness for the wrongs of life. There came compassion for the earth, for how it holds our journeys, sorrows, pains, wars, and tragedies. Love for the earth welled up, along with the thought that it could truly become a place we all love; a place where we love and care for all things.

Yes, today was a beautiful reminder that being human is rare and beautiful – it is a unique privilege.

What was your experience?

DAY 66

God, what would you have me say, do, or be like today?

Be patient.
    Endure your frustrations patiently and
    release them to my care.

By doing so you will receive grace
and your spirit will transform.

Know there is great love always flowing.
   Open yourself
and allow love to enter your depths.
Breathe it in deeply and
receive it with humility and thanks.

Carry your burdens quietly today
and remember how blessed you really are.

Remember that love is patient and kind.
It does not hold on to wrongs done to you.

Give thanks for all things today
– and let yourself be loved.

DAY 67

God, what would you have me say, do, or be like today?

Be still....

In doing so, you will know I am God.

Stillness of mind allows stillness
of body and emotions.

Be calm and know I hold all things;
know all is within me, and I am in you.

Let anxiety become peace
as it rests in my love and care.

Let joy rise in you like a radiant sun.
Be bright and fresh;
give warmth and light to the world.

In your speech and actions
let this light shine.
    It will be seen.

Be still...
and know I am...
    and I am in you ...
        now
and always.

DAY 68

God, what would you have me say, do, or be like today?

Remember
you live in heaven's domain.
The kingdom of heaven is in you.

Its energy surrounds you.
Let it wash over you and penetrate.
    Bathe in its love.
Bask in its light.

You cannot make mistakes here.
All you say and do is within its grace.

Your talents, skills, curiosities
– even your styles of work and play –
are blessed gifts to you.

I give you your own works to perform,
    and I look for a ripe return.

Offer yourself to my love and care today,
continuously.
I will guide you and work with you,
    in you, and through you.

This relationship is the divine exchange.

DAY 69

God, what would you have me say, do, or be like today?

Be attentive.

Show love, care, and
    concern for the welfare of others.

Be complimentary. Notice the things
    that are precious signs of love or kindness.
        Tell someone that you notice.

Be joyful,
    even if your joy is silent and shows only
        in your eyes or your smile.

Show your trust in divine guidance.
    Move with grace and comfort.
    Know you are where you are supposed to be,
        doing what you are supposed to be doing.

Enjoy moving in the flow of divine guidance.
    Sense its gentle nudging.

Appreciate nature as you go through the day.
    Listen to birdsong,
        feel the wind and rain,
            splash in puddles,
                let the sun kiss your face.

Notice the colours and aromas of the earth
        and know that you are part of nature –
and part of the nature of God.

DAY 70

God, what would you have of me today?

I would have your heart of love,
    your outpouring of compassion and care.

You are about others today.

Give. Let others feel your availability.
There will be time and room for your own work.

Share yourself.
    Be a beautiful soul.

    Serve others today and
do not hold back your kindness.
How you make others feel is what is important.

    Be beautiful, and see how the world
responds.
Let your heart-forces bless all who cross your
path.

EVENING REFLECTION

I felt guided to ask a question that has come up a
few times before: *What would you have of me?* It dif-
fers from *What should I do, or say, or be like?* in that
it implies that the Creator can receive and use our
open hearts for divine purposes.

Today was a wonderful demonstration of this.

A friend needed support in dealing with a person from
whom she wanted to distance herself. The courage
and self-compassion that my friend had to display in
order to say *No* was tremendous.

It was a heavy workday, but there is nothing like
being there for someone in need. Letting my friend
know that I recognized the strength it took to stand
strong, encouraged and affirmed her.

I got back to my work with a sense of having been, at
least for a while, a beautiful soul for someone else.

That is a hard feeling to beat.

DAY 71

God, what would you have me say or do today?

Do what brings peace.
    Let your words bring peace.

    Now here comes the tricky part.

You do not know what will bring peace to
another;
    you must trust my guidance.

You also might not know what will bring *you*
peace.

The only real peace is found in total surrender –
    to divine wisdom, love, and care.
Only I can hold your uncertainty, pain, and doubt
    and transform them to perfect peace.

To act peacefully is to serve me.
To speak peacefully is to let go
    of your ego and allow a higher mind to
emerge.

Let divinity in today...and peace will come out.

    Will you do this?

DAY 72

God, what would you have me say, do, or be like today?

Be honest.
> Do not hide from your feelings.
> > Do not pretend.

Shine as you are.
> See yourself.

Take stock of what is in you.
> Trust my spirit in this endeavour,
> > knowing that I love you.

See your light, your shadows,
> and your dark places.
Lift them
> to my purifying love and understanding.
Release yourself
> to my care and service.

Be true to yourself today.
Be genuine, and be so without guilt, fear, or
hesitation.

You are a holy being who is still growing
and who has much goodness to share.

Honesty will serve you well.

Trust –
and be honest.

EVENING REFLECTION

When this guidance came through, I again did not have a clue as to how it would play out. It didn't seem to be what I needed. At least that is what I thought. I wanted to guide my guidance.

Well, it didn't take long (again) to see the wisdom in the day's message. Maybe two minutes went by, and then, in the most surprising way, I was confronted with the challenge of honesty. It came in the simple form of the question, *What do I want to do next?*

Then came the *shoulds*... Then came the crazy thoughts: *I could just jump in the car and drive off to some other state.* Then came the guidance: *Be honest.* I took time to pause and sift through the mind's barrage of thoughts and connect with my heart. And then I knew what I truly wanted to do next. I wanted to work on a board game I was developing. Now to many this may not qualify to be among life's *important* things, but it is what I wanted to spend time doing. And I did. It was fun. I moved the development of the game forward a bit and gained great satisfaction, which I carried through the day!

When the guidance – *Be honest* – came in it was so clear, even surprisingly so. Learning to hear God speak within me is an exercise in letting go and allowing my heart and intuition to take centre stage. I have to trust the letting go and the receiving – no matter how surprising the message.

DAY 73

God, what would you have of me today?

I would have your focus.
Surrender your will and want to me today.

Then I can accomplish in you, with you,
and through you the highest aims of your day.

What you feel as tension is the edge of pride.
Let go and allow me to lead you today.

      Trust my love.
      Trust that my wisdom knows what is best.

Have courage. It is only for today.
Tomorrow will offer its own agreement.

Lean into my spirit – keep leaning into me.
  We will be one.
You will feel me as you surrender and let go.

Fear not.
Enjoy the day's journey while I guide.

DAY 74

God, what would you have me say or do today?

Speak as an angel.
      Move as a being of light.

As you live into this today
you will connect with what you really are:
an angel of light in human form.

It is not unbelievable.
      It is you.

      Angels serve God,
and in your highest consciousness
      you do also.

Move past your egoic self
and present your authentic spirit to the world.
      That is what this day is for.

Be an angel of light on the earth today
and you will bless the world
with the wonder of your being.

EVENING REFLECTION

Let's just say I was not an angel all day.

On several occasions throughout the day I lost patience. However, when I remembered the guidance I was able to connect with the angel in me and the light that I hold. I had what I would call a series of saves, like in soccer or hockey when the goalie grabs the ball or puck and prevents the other team from scoring. Or even in baseball, when the closing pitcher comes on to save the game and get the win for the team.

My saves were more of the soccer and hockey variety than baseball though. See, in baseball the closer comes on to protect a lead. I was not leading. And I certainly was not following – not until I remembered the guidance. Then I was able to let go of my ego and watch the divinity in me employ my mind, heart, and soul. I became softer, kinder, more patient and loving – instantly! More wisdom flowed into what I said. It was an incredible difference, and one that made all the difference!

How did you do with this one?

DAY 75

God, what would you have me say, do, or be like today?

Be flexible.
    Go with the flow without fuss.
    Be adaptable and easygoing.
Relax and breathe deeply;
feel the blessing of your life.
    Do your work joyfully;
be grateful for your skills and talents.

Watch life unfold today and see what comes.
Accept it all knowing that divinity holds you.

    Enjoy who you are today.
    Find time to be alone to sense the
       remarkable gift of your presence.
    Try to stay in this energy field all day,
       no matter what transpires.

Peace is always yours to claim. Live in it today.

EVENING REFLECTION

Today I began a project I thought would take at least a couple of months of steady work to complete. I worked with joy all day, off and on, and later into the wee hours of the morning. So this reflection is being written very late.

Because I wanted to focus on the project and work without disturbance, my ability to be flexible with my schedule was challenged, especially once I got on a roll. At one point I felt guided to call my mother. Later there came the nudge to call a contact about a business idea. And still later I felt the need to spend time with my wife and then have a text conversation with my daughter.

Remembering the guidance, I let it all flow. I was flexible, adaptable, and easygoing. When I finally got space to work into the night, a most surprising thing occurred. I finished the project! I completed in less than 24 hours something I thought would take months. But I worked with joy and appreciated the skills that allowed me to do the work. I worked in a state of joy and peace and the ideas flowed without tiring me out.

It was a demonstration of how going with the flow can yield divine results that surprise and amaze.

What was your experience with this guidance today?

DAY 76

God, what would you have me say, do, or be like today?

Be the loving person that you are.

As love is the primary power of life,
it shines from deep inside.
    See its light flow into the spaces around you.
    Let it guide your speech and movements.
Love the world by looking upon it with
    appreciation and joy.
Feel your whole being pulse as you
    send forth blessing after blessing
        because you love.
And as you love,
    receive the grace of my spirit,
for you are a holy being –
divine,
    shining,
        and blessed.

EVENING REFLECTION

Today's guidance reminded me to be the way I would like to think I am anyway: loving. That said, we could all use a little on-field coaching at times. Today's guidance was just that. It was also a beautiful guidance to live into. And I did pretty well – for a while. However, a strong challenge came at the end of the day. I was very tired and ready to go to bed when someone knocked on my door. It was a neighbour who needed help with a matter he couldn't resolve.

Well, I didn't jump at the chance to be of assistance, knowing I had an early morning to look forward to. However, my inner coach kept saying to me, "Be the loving person that you are." This really helped me to remain in my love. I endured more easily the strong desire to say no and go to bed because I knew the loving thing to do was to help. Of course, sometimes the loving thing to do is to say no and go to bed. But I knew I could be of service and that the bed would still be there afterwards. So I listened and offered suggestions and was thanked for my understanding.

I then went right to bed and fell asleep quickly. And I slept rather well, sensing that I had done the right thing. I wonder how I would have slept if I had turned the person away? Glad I didn't have to find out.

How did you do today?

DAY 77

God, what would you have me say, do, or be like today?

Listen.
> Listen to everything.
Speak little.
> Do less.

Listen.
> Listen to your own life.
Listen to your quietest thoughts
> and hear what is being voiced
>> in the deepest realms of your being.

Listen.
> Listen to nature.
Listen to wind, the trees rustling,
> the buzzes and flaps of flying creatures,
> the quiet of a frozen lake.

Listen.
> Listen with all your senses.
Do not have expectation; just listen.
> You may even hear the sound of sound...
> and of my love.

Listen.
> You may hear just what you need to hear.
Something is waiting
> just for you to hear today.
>> Listen.

EVENING REFLECTION

I am writing this evening reflection at 9:57 a.m.!

I find listening with my whole being – with all my senses – amazing!

I am sitting in a church with my wife, preparing to spend the day listening to lectures and poetry by a well-known writer. I am listening deeply, and I can hear many things. I hear my own fear, my knee-jerk responses, my subtle judgments, and my guilt about them. My hope sounds as a feeling tone.

Ears hear, fingers touch, noses smell, mouths taste, eyes see. Our senses are connections. They connect us to the world we are in and to the world in us. None of our senses is limited to the small physical range we may assign to it, and paying attention to wider, more expansive sensing may lead to some wonderful experiences. Tasting a lover with your eyes might lead to a delicious kiss; smelling the ocean with your feet might lead to a headlong dive into a wave. There are no limits to the ways we can experience and employ our senses except those we place on them.

I heard today in many ways and modes. I even heard God loving me, and I think I heard the sound of sound.

DAY 78

God, what would you have me say, do, or be like today?

Do things that show love.
Say something to build up another.
    Be a source of goodness.

Do not allow negativity to thwart your efforts.

Consider any test a blessing in disguise.
Breathe in, smile, and know
    the divine in you
can conquer any challenge.

Speak with love today.
Act with kindness.
    Put others first.
And be thankful for the power of love
that allows this outpouring of divinity from you
today.

DAY 79

God, what would you have of me today?

I would have your peace.

Let the sound of your voice,
the cadence of your speech,
the movements and mannerisms of your body
exude peace and calm.

Be at peace today.

All is perfect. All is happening as it should.
Nothing is out of place.
Nothing.

    Can you believe this for just this one day?
      Try. Relax.

You cannot make all things right anyway,
so breathe, and be at peace.
You will be ushered into a different experience
of day – of experience itself.

Let peace guide you, fill you, and flow from you,
and you will see my peace in all things.

DAY 80

God, what would you have me say, do, or be like today?

Be like water.
Conform to the shape of the day holding you.
Follow the path of least resistance.
    Rest when the opportunity presents itself,
        even if for only a moment at a time,
            even for just one or two deep breaths.

        Give the journey of this day to me.
    I will direct you in all your ways.

    I know your path.
Let go and see how easily you can move
    when you trust me to guide you.

        Get ready for a beautiful journey today.
            Breathe deeply, relax, and enjoy the peace
that comes with knowing my grace and love are
with you.

Let go and trust...
    Move and flow with me today.

Today almost everything I didn't want to happen, happened. Nothing went as planned or hoped.

Suffice to say being like water and conforming to the shape of the day was difficult at best. I wanted more control, which in water terms meant flooding and overpowering the natural contours of the day's banks, so to speak.

Today also revealed that I was carrying more than a little frustration and resentment regarding a challenging circumstance. The tone of my inner being was not sounding as pretty notes! As I couldn't seem to get rid of the feelings, I decided to go and work out. Sometimes physical exercise helps me to dissipate unwanted emotions. And it did help. It also helped that I followed the guidance's encouragement to go the way of least resistance. I didn't pick an argument when I could have; I didn't announce my frustration or resentment; I didn't act out. I gave the day to God – *many times* – and went on. And yes, it was challenging to do that. I think some days are just that way.

Guess what? Everything worked out by about 5:00 p.m.!

I am reminded to "let patience have her perfect work."

Today I also took moments to rest, which was helpful, especially in terms of renewing my energy, strength, and inner peace. This in turn allowed me to keep conforming to the shape of the day, letting go and letting God.

The day's journey was not so beautiful on my part. But when I did give things to God, it got exponentially easier. I will come back to this one again. It is a doozie!

How was it for you?

DAY 81

God, what would you have me say or do today?

Speak words that enliven everyone you meet
today.
　　Speak words that affirm the best in them
　　and show your love and care.

Reach out with your heart.
　　Your love is powerful.
　　Let it come forth in all its beauty and grace.

Today, do for others.
　　Be accommodating and flexible.
Take less note of your personal interests.
　　Be selfless.

Know that your own needs will be met,
 even as you seek to meet
　　the needs of others.

Enjoy your freedom from your self today,
as you become a source of blessing for others.

DAY 82

**God, what would you have me say, do, or be like
today?**

Be my representative today.

　　Stay in my energy.
　　　Let it continuously empower you.

　　Let me see through your eyes and
　　speak through your mouth.
　Let me infuse your thoughts
with my divine radiance.

　　Be calm, loving, and sure
　　as you walk and serve as
an agent of light.

　　Be joyful and life-giving
　　in all endeavours.

Will you?

DAY 83

God, what would you have me say, do, or be like today?

Be both rock and feather:
    strong, solid, grounded;
light, sure, able to go where *ruah*
leads you.

Be firm in trusting me as the foundation of your
being today.
Trust the inner leaning you sense.
        I am there.

Let nothing take you by surprise.
Maintain a steady, gentle demeanor.

As we live this day together,
you will feel my grace and love.
Speak to others with this same grace and love.
Receive my blessing and pass it on.

Move in grace and love today,
and know that all is unfolding
as it should.

Let's enjoy our day together.
        I am with you, always.

EVENING REFLECTION

Because there is such depth to the wisdom of each guidance, one line or concept sometimes becomes a focal point. Today I focused on giving blessing. Giving blessing is a component of compassion. Compassion is a powerful energy, and genuinely extending compassion to others can open doors to connection and healing.

Today's guidance reminded me to get out of myself and let my own stuff retreat into the background. It can be a great relief to immerse in the act of caring for others. When people feel that we are truly present for them, the opportunity for more intimate sharing is created. The conversations, interactions, and trust that came my way today were tremendously satisfying. My own personal challenges are still there waiting for me. But compassion's payoff is that our own problems become smaller as our soul expands through caring about others.

(Later in the evening)
As my wife and I were preparing for a date night of dinner and a movie, she received a call from a friend in crisis. We both knew she had to go. Date night would have to wait. As she drove off to help her friend, I remembered the final reminder in today's guidance: that all was unfolding as it should. This helped me to let go and let God.

DAY 84

God, what would you have me say and do today?

Forgive.

Begin with yourself.
Every time you need forgiveness,
    you reaffirm your humanity.
It does not mean that you haven't moved forward
    in your spiritual growth or evolution.
You are simply experiencing
            another point of growth.

So celebrate that discovery and forgive yourself.
Have compassion, understanding,
            and love for your journey.

Forgive others for any perceived offences,
    no matter how small the slight.
Look at your own ego and love it as you would
            a vulnerable child.

Know that the actions of others
are never quite as you might think.
            Give it all to God.
Take a deep breath and move on,
and give thanks for the opportunity
to grow further into your own divinity.

            Forgive.

DAY 85

God, what would you have me say, do, or be like today?

Be calm,
anxious about nothing.
Flow in the direction of my gentle leading.

Breathe as smoothly and deeply as you can,
and stay conscious of your breath,
especially during challenging situations.

Let your mind relax and be held in my care,
and know that the needs of the day will be met.
Take time to be, without agenda
or need to accomplish.

Be aware of your greater self.
Feel the transcendence of your soul –
that part of you that watches,
with peaceful detachment,
the unfolding daily human drama.

Even if you do this for only moments at a time,
you will be rewarded with feelings of peace and
calm.

Sink into the resources the heavenly realm offers.
Sense the deep well of joy that underlies your cares,
and connect to this refreshment.
Rest here as much as you can today
and enjoy the renewal of your soul, mind, and
spirit.

DAY 86

God, what would you have me say, do, or be like today?

Speak honestly and softly.
Trust the unfolding without flinching.
   Keep your ego out of the way.
Divinity proceeds through an open heart.

Stay aware of the bigger context.
Be happy knowing there is a higher order
of wisdom, agency, and revelation
working things to a greater good.

Relax and keep breathing consciously.
Stay calm and trusting.
   Love whomever you meet today.
     Be humble.
   Listen.
Be open.
Be at peace with all that transpires.

EVENING REFLECTION

Part of my day contained a meeting at which I had to deliver some sobering information concerning legal matters. I knew there was a possibility that the information might bring to a halt a project I have been working on with two other people for over two years. Today's guidance fit the needs of the meeting perfectly. I even read it aloud to my partners when the conversation got to the "big gulp" stage.

I think it helped us get over the wall of facing certain failure to a place where we could engage creative thinking, go back to square one, and look at what we had to see if anything was still useful. It gave us the wherewithal to make room for new ideas. And it gave us cause to keep our hearts open, which allowed divine creativity and a larger perspective to guide us.

After the meeting, my wife and I went to a new restaurant to talk over some marketing ideas. As we were talking, two acquaintances saw us and came over to our table. We had been on a roll with ideas, but we interrupted the flow to be present with the folks who had shown up. Well, as we allowed the unfolding without flinching (much), it turned out that the conversation yielded even more ideas to explore and riff on.

So again, the Divine guides and acts throughout our day – and even *gets in our business* (to use a colloquial expression)!

DAY 87

God, what would you have me say or do today?

Speak with genuine compassion.
Act with grace and beauty.

It may be challenging,
but manifesting these virtues
brings blessing to your soul
and the souls of others.

Remember –
spiritual growth is not achieved without pain.

Where kindness is difficult to offer,
the strength of your willingness to love
determines the course of your actions.

The perceived imperfections of life provide a
perfect way to mature as a divine being.

Speak humbly when you do not want to.
Be silent when what you would say is not kind.
Sacrifice your ego's triumph
to your spirit's humility.
Love beyond your present
boundaries today,
and you will find those boundaries
expanding.

This is what it feels like to evolve
and grow into the power of your own divinity.

You can do it if that is what you want.
Is it?

EVENING REFLECTION

Moments that test a person's resolve to love beyond their present ability can be surprisingly difficult, especially if they involve being humble. Living out love in its greatest form takes intent and determination and involves lots of work on oneself. Testing moments usually come during life's tense, emotional events: in the heated throes of another's hatred toward you, or during someone's anger at feeling betrayed by you, or when being blamed for another's disappointment that life has not given them what they think it should. There is an endless supply of scenarios that challenge one's resolve to act with grace, beauty, and genuine compassion, and love past one's present boundaries. We can rarely achieve it alone. It usually takes a power beyond most people's resources. It usually takes grace.

When I have been caught in the throes of powerful emotions that challenge my resolve to love, and then managed, with God's grace and strength, to push through my very human emotions to a better space beyond ego, I marvel at the landscape I find there. I find peace and beauty of a magnitude I have not known before. To reach this place, I start by letting go. I drop the garments and accoutrements of ego and stand naked before the Divine. Then I get honest about myself and confess. When I do this, I find there is no need for covering. There is no need for anger, jealousy, getting back at, or any of the myriad tricks humans use to manipulate people. I realize that everyone is doing the best they can. This intrinsic knowing is the basis for forgiveness. Love and forgiveness are made a little easier when I realize that each person is innocent and doing his or her best, even if I think they should know better and do better. This includes loving and forgiving myself.

DAY 88

God, what would you have me say, do, or be like today?

Be a source of joy!

Laugh,
    play,
        and let humour rule the day.

    Let your spirit dance.

Be lighthearted.
    Let your eyes twinkle!

Allow happiness to have its way
    in your soul.

Turn adversity into comedy,
    and problems into parody.

Be surprised by your own capacity
    to create
        joy!

And watch what happens.

Be fun.
Have fun.

Create joy
    in your own life
        today!

DAY 89

God, what would you have me say and do today?

Today,
    be aware of compassion.

Extend care toward others.
    Listen with sensitivity and respond with encouraging words and a comforting tone.

    This will minimize your own challenges
and give you a chance to rest.
    Then you can step outside yourself
and be available and present
    for another.

The nourishment you will receive
    is food for your soul.

Enjoy!

DAY 90

God, what would you have me say, do, or be like today?

Continue becoming attuned and sensitive
to my spirit.

Pay attention to your heart.
Hear with it.
Listen with non-judgmental ease.
Look out on the world through it.
Effortlessly extend your compassion from it.
Speak from it.
Say words that are loving, kind, and
encouraging.

As you do these things,
aware of my divine presence,
you live the day as a blessed entity
who transmits love and divine grace to all people
– even when you are silent.

It takes little effort to bless.
You only need a big heart, open to me.

Are you paying attention?

DAY 91

God, what would you have me say, do, or be like today?

You are manifesting more of your divinity.
You are living into your potential to bless.

Today, rest in the knowledge that you are exactly
where you are supposed to be.

Enjoy letting your light
touch the world around you.

You don't need to "do" or "say" anything.

Just be you.
You are enough.

Be in the world as you are –
holy, blessed, and full of divine light.

DAY 92

God, what would you have me say, do, or be like today?

Be joy and humour and laughter.

Frame all you say and do in joy.
Joy heals and blesses all.

Laughter is one of life's sweetest sounds.
Laugh, and make others laugh.

Let humour enter your perspective today.

All cares and concerns
can be lightened by humour and joy.

    Let your joy and humour be genuine.

As joy guides you,
know that I am within you,
filling you with my own JOY...
laughing inside your laughter.

DAY 93

God, what would you have me say, do, or be like today?

Be kind and gentle,
    loving and fair.

Be attentive
    without being intrusive.

Remember to listen
    with your heart.

Receive help and love from others
    without being defensive.

Be firm when necessary
    but have compassion.

Be a joy
    to be around.

Let divine love of life show
    in all you do and say today.

Receive joy from others
    and let it inspire your own.

EVENING REFLECTION

This guidance came the morning I was leaving the country for a family vacation. I enjoy travelling immensely but it can also come with long lineups and lots of tedious waiting. To be joy and love may seem like a fluffy, corny, hippy-ish kind of line, but it *isn't*. It is a spiritual challenge that can make anyone look like a work in progress – especially on long travel days.

How'd you do?

DAY 94

God, what would you have me say, do, or be like today?

Be receptive.
Be aware of your connection to me.
Together we will live this day
as a prayer.

Do not rush or hurry today.
    There is an easy rhythm
        of divine flow awaiting you.
    Find it and stay in it,
no matter how events
        rush at you.

Move slowly with ease and grace.
    Relax your body.
        Breathe deeply and with gratitude.
    There is space to accomplish all
that needs to be done.

Relax and trust.
Relax and trust.

EVENING REFLECTION

It is hard to be receptive when it means having to hear what we don't want to hear. Today was one of those days. News came that a cousin had died while returning home from her daughter's funeral. While this news was painful to hear, the woman who is the mother and grandmother of those lost had to absorb the deaths of two women in her direct lineage in as many weeks. Speaking with her was to hear raw pain.

Amid the grief and sadness, the guidance helped me to remember to live the day as a prayer and give all that happens to God's care. When tragedy strikes it is easy to question Divinity. Sometimes we don't want to connect with a god that allows bad things to happen to good people.

I decided that I would try to follow what Divinity sent my way through the guidance and stay in divine flow no matter how the day rushed at me. I still had to work and run errands and be with my own immediate family. I tried to relax and move with ease and grace while holding sadness and questions. To relax and trust was a bit difficult today. It was the reminder to live in gratitude that eventually won out though. Loving memories and thankfulness triumphed over despair.

What did this day hold for you?

DAY 95

God, what would you have me say, do, or be like today?

Count it all joy today!

Practice seeing blessings,
knowing that God loves you and all others.

Should something occur today
that you see as unfortunate,
connect your mind to me
as the source of higher understanding
and see what may be revealed.

Remember that I am working for the good of all.

I bless creation with love and support,
although you are free to reject this.

Today, be an ambassador of love, joy, and peace.
See challenges as opportunities for growth.

Do not buy into any of your ego's ploys
to get you to live under its rule.
Let go...and allow my spirit to guide you.

Do not defend yourself today.
Be kind and patient.
Be a wise and compassionate teacher.
Be a source of joy and peace.

Do not let anything get in the way of your efforts.
Tests will come.
Be strong.

Today, you have all you need to grow,
to withstand challenge,
to transform adversity into triumph,
to share wisdom, love, and light.
Count it all joy!

DAY 96

God, what would you have me say, do, or be like today?

Be quiet.
When you speak, use a calm, soft tone.

When you keep quiet, you will begin to hear
the sounds of your soul.

The soul knows what it needs,
but you must let it speak to you.

Quiet calms the surface chatter and
allows a deeper awareness.
Speak and act from this awareness today.

Awareness holds wisdom and power.
You will sense more clarity and purpose.

See how long you can stay in this place.

In this place you are more like
the real you...
the YOU
beneath the you.

Be this person today.

EVENING REFLECTION

Today was a fairly routine day. Not much happened. But the interactions I had were particularly enjoyable because I slowed down. I spoke and moved in a relaxed manner, without forcing my own agenda. I allowed conversations and events to filter past the surface processors of my brain, past my emotional filters, and into the depths of my soul and spirit. This takes paying attention to heart and soul.

I discerned a difference in my personal power as a result of paying attention. This power is different from force. Power is the unseen divine essence you exude and present naturally. It is spiritual and cannot be evoked by will. It is recognized through inner awareness and brings with it much grace. Force is expressed through the will of the ego and is experienced through the senses. It has to do with control, manipulation, and pride, and calibrates low in terms of spiritual energy. Power allows wisdom to be engaged. It allows me to respond with integrity and to act with love, joy, and care.

How did you do with this one today?

DAY 97

God, what would you have me say, do, or be like today?

Be brave.
Have courage – a big heart – and speak from it.
There is no need to fear the future or the present.

Trust that there is no failure.
There cannot be failure
when all is contained in my spirit.

When working with others let my divinity
fill the spaces that separate you.

Do not hesitate to mention me.
Be ready to acknowledge, in all things,
my presence and participation.

You are divine.
May all you say and do today reflect this reality.
Let divinity flow through
all that you consider and create.

DAY 98

God, what would you have me say, do, or be like today?

Be like a tree planted firmly
so that no matter what happens
you are securely rooted
in my peace, power, and sureness.

No matter what the day brings,
do not be dismayed.
Remember where your spirit and soul are rooted,
and go there whenever you need to gain strength
or find calm.

Take time to deepen your grounding
through prayer and meditation.
Stay aware of my presence with you and in you.

Thoughts and emotions may sway you,
but keep your faith firmly planted in my love.

      And remember my gift of connection.

You are not alone...
You are created in love...
You can receive spiritual nourishment
and power for life.

Live in this miracle.
Ask for what you want and need today.
And claim it!

DAY 99

God, what would you have me say and do today?

Do what feels right and good.
      Say what feels honest and nourishing.

As you honour these things,
      you will open the door to other virtues.

Just breathe easily and stay attuned
to joyful spirit bubbling deep within.

Your joy is my joy.
      Let joy do its work within you.
        Let it flow through you
          and touch all your endeavours.
Be joyful even during quiet solitude.

Yes – today, do what feels right and good.
Say what feels honest and nourishing.

That makes a beautiful day.

DAY 100

God, what would you have of me today?

I would have your keen vision.
Keep looking deeper into me.

See all things as manifestations of divinity.
Trees, mountains, clouds, wild animals,
people interacting...
    ...I am in their midst.

Hear what I am saying to you.
Sense my guidance.
Do not look away from me.
    As we gaze into each other,
you will flow with the works of my
working and we will create blessing together.

EVENING REFLECTION

This was a beautiful challenge. It felt amazing to stay conscious and see Divinity everywhere, even in the cracks on the sidewalk. It was fun to try to see "deeply" into all things. It made me focus my consciousness differently and attune my awareness to a different frequency. I felt more awake and alert. Ultimately, today's practice was one that let me know that I can home in on God's presence within all things.

That alone made the day's guidance worthwhile.

DAY 101

God, what would you have of me today?

I would have your welcoming spirit.
Be open to what comes to you today.
Imagine your arms open wide,
    and your heart also.

Whether challenge or joy, be receptive to all,
for I use all things for your spiritual movement.

Look for the lesson or wisdom in the day's events.
Bring them into yourself
    and let them sink in.

Be joyful for the opportunity to grow and mature.
Do not fear the hard parts of the day.
Bring them into my divine energy,
    that they may bear fruit for you.
Be welcoming.

DAY 102

God, what would you have of me today?

I would have more of your time.

When the scriptures speak of me as a jealous god, it means that nothing should take a position of greater importance than our connection.

Spending time in prayer, meditation, and contemplation yields gifts that are not easily gained otherwise.

I would have more of your time today, to deepen you in me.

Can you,
    will you,
        find the time?
        Today,
      tomorrow...
Always?

EVENING REFLECTION

Every once in a while, and more often than I would like, I allow my time communing with the Divine to be squeezed. I try to be consciously aware of my connection to God every moment of every day, but like most people, I'm just not there. Job, family, paying bills, driving kids to activities, cooking – LIFE– all make it easy to let time pass without focusing on the Creator. The pace of life is one reason why people go on spiritual retreat where they can spend more concentrated time staying conscious of Divinity.

Remember that even Christ went to a high mountain to find some alone time with the Almighty. So in lieu of always being in a very high state spiritually, we just need to make some time to connect in a conscious way with our Creator. That time spent in purposeful communing is like no other experience. Besides, who wants a jealous God? Not me.

DAY 103

God, what would you have me be like today?

Be like a cool wind
and a soft breeze.

May your words soothe.
May your temperament be calm and gentle.

Let others' air blow through you
like wind through the trees.

Listen loudly;
speak quietly.

Be there for others.
    I am here for you.

Watch the day
with joy and gratitude as it unfolds,
and it will be one beautiful day.

EVENING REFLECTION

The part of the guidance that was most potent for me today was about letting the air of other people blow through me like wind through trees. For me that meant not letting people get to me, push my buttons, or get on my nerves. I had to not take things personally even though it seemed that more people than usual threw out their stuff toward me today! I laughed almost every time it happened because I realized that the guidance had opened the door of opportunity to the challenge.

Doing the other things in the guidance also helped me to let things blow through. I could be a cool breeze *and* a soft wind. They may seem like the same thing to some but they are actually complementary. At least they were for me. My actions were the cool breeze and my words the soft wind.

Listen loudly? Now there's a challenge. To hear the harmonics in a person's tone, to hear what they are saying beneath what they are saying is to listen loudly. And committing to *not defending myself* allowed me softer speech and more ease of being because my emotions were not riled up.

To the extent I was able to be present for others today, I did feel a sense that God was with me. And that made it...a beautiful day!

How was yours?

DAY 104

God, what would you have me say, do, or be like today?

Be warm like the sun
and gently radiate
love, kindness, and compassion.

Be light...
quiet and bright.
Remember that your power to shine emanates
from love.

Shine light on whatever obstructs you
and transform it through my grace and power.

Speak from your joyful centre;
act from your compassionate heart.

As you love others today,
    let me love you.
        Okay?

EVENING REFLECTION

As gentle a guidance as this may seem, it proved very instructive – and challenging. I say challenging because today the guidance made me aware of blocks to the light as they came up. They were mostly small blocks, but nonetheless they kept my inner light from shining as brightly as it might have.

For instance, I ran into an acquaintance I don't connect well with. I was aware that I wanted to avoid a conversation but doing so would have been obvious and awkward. So I shone a light on it, walked through my own shadow, and felt myself let my light come through. That took willingness, and I wasn't sure I could let go of my ego and humble myself. But trying allowed the grace of God to do most of the work for me. Divinity's love changed me in that moment and I had a sustained, normal conversation with my acquaintance.

I was aware of not being in a mood to be polite and easygoing today, which was amusing because that goes against my general nature. But I allowed myself to feel it without judging it. I shone an inner light on it and I ended up being very accommodating to those whose paths I crossed.

I let God love me, which meant letting the cracks and crevices of my personality and mood be infused with divinity. The easiest way for me to describe the how of it is to say that I let go of all things negative, even if I was enjoying them. You can draw in grace by humbling yourself and asking the Divine to help you. This changes your energy and allows a powerful connection to the transformative grace and power of God.

DAY 105

God, what would you have me say, do, or be like today?

Be beautiful.
This means be virtuous.
Let honesty and peace
    guide your words and actions.

Be courteous and confident in all situations.
Know that you belong to the human community.
Let self-doubt rest today.

        You are enough.

Let it be okay to be where you are in life today.

Be humble about your achievements and
have compassion for yourself when you fail.

Be graceful and gracious today,
    like a wave
    gently rolling across the ocean of life.

Treat others as special guests in your life.

Move through the day knowing you are held
in my divine energy of love and acceptance.

Love with the ease of one who is
loved unconditionally.

See how you are blessed.

Yes...be beautiful.

EVENING REFLECTION

This call to be beautiful has come up a time or two. And I find it has become a favourite guidance. We all want to be beautiful, I think. And this guidance affirms that all of us can be beautiful. This has nothing to do with our looks and everything to do with our choices and intentions. Greeting the busy grocery store cashier kindly, driving mindfully and looking out for others, looking people in the eye and smiling while speaking to them: doing these things with ease comes from knowing we belong and are where we are supposed to be.

Beauty allows the best in us to exude effortlessly. Accepting our beauty as a son or daughter of God transcends our ego and taps into the truth of who we are – who we all are. It is a place of no competition, no better-than. It is a place where divinity emerges and shines through us, moment by moment – because we can't help it.

It is who we are. Beautiful.

DAY 106

God, what would you have me say, do, or be like today?

Be like a gently flowing, meandering river.
Let your experiences
deepen your soul and widen your heart.

Carry the waters of joy, refreshment,
    and love.

Let love deepen you.

Let maturity move you through the day's twists and turns,
    however challenging they may be.

Be aware that you emerge from my divine outpouring,
and flow toward that which receives all.

What you are now is a gift to all.

    What will you become?

EVENING REFLECTION

I can never accurately predict how a guidance will play out, or how it will connect with the day. But it always does connect, and usually in ways that prove amazing.

How can a person be like a gentle meandering river?! As I took in this image, I had to laugh. But as I walked around, I was able to be like that. And I was not pretending. I could feel my energy flowing.

Moreover, the word gentle really helped keep me that way. This was helpful because I had a meeting that was a turning point in a creative process that had been going on for two and a half years. As we delved into aspects of the radical changes to come, and as feelings were brought to the table, I noticed I was somehow able to let the tension and intensity of the experience deepen my soul and widen my heart. How did the "let" happen? I allowed feelings that were coming up to touch me deeply as they passed. I didn't filter or judge them, and I found that just listening with acceptance deepened my capacity to hold others where they are.

I matured in those moments (we never reach maturity if we want to keep growing), and when I spoke in the meeting I brought in what was useful from my own life without being pushy, defensive, or arrogant. The meeting, and the rest of the day, flowed – meandered – with a beautiful rhythm that seemed graced by God.

How was your meandering today?

DAY 107

God, what would you have me say and do today?

Do what benefits your physical body.
Eat wisely – with conscious appreciation.

Feel your strength and well-being.
Commit to tending the areas of your body
that need support and exercise.

Appreciate the gift of your body
and delight in what it allows you to do.

Take pleasure in the way you move.
Notice the mannerisms of your hands,
and how you sit and stand.

Be grateful for your body;
it is your conduit of experience
and expression.

Be great friends with it today.
Love it.

Give thanks for the physical body
you have been wrapped in
for this human experience.

With appreciation and gratitude,
enjoy the privilege and beauty of your body
today.

EVENING REFLECTION

Today's guidance was a tall order. It spoke to me all day in everything I did. Though exercise is a regular part of my life, today's reminder served to make me attentive to the spiritual nature of the human body. It is a gift to each of us. If we go out for a walk, we can enjoy and notice how we move. Paying attention to the areas of our body that are usually forgotten about, unless they are in pain, can be a wonderful exercise in befriending our own being. When do we honour our elbows and knees? Our heels? Or the lines and wrinkles on our hands and feet?

We take in our earthly experiences through our bodies. There are things we can do only because we are embodied. So today I drank a glass of water and put my total attention on how I swallowed, how the coolness felt going down my throat, and even how I held the cup.

In the evening, my wife and I put on our monthly event where we put people in tap shoes and lead them in movement, with an eye toward connection on a spiritual level. I emphasized being thankful for our bodies and paying attention to the parts of ourselves we may not think of so much. We then ate a healthy meal together and talked about the obvious and subtle connections between body and spirit.

How did today's guidance speak to your day?

DAY 108

God, what would you have me say, do, or be like today?

You have already done it.
You have been responsive to the leading of my spirit.
You have followed your inner guidance.

You have allowed your own plans to be subsumed under my divine guidance.
You have sought out and listened to the still, quiet voice.

Because of your willingness to engage my will, others will be fed spiritually.

Rest well in the knowledge that today you have communed with me and responded to my love; love that holds and guides all.

DAY 109

God, what would you have me say and do today?

Say what is enlivening!
Do what is uplifting!

Focus on inviting others
into your unconditional love and support.

Reach out to someone in a special way today.

Extend the beauty of your spirit
by staying connected to the source of beauty
and smiling with your whole being.

Let love softly emanate from your heart.

Enjoy the beauty of all beings today.

Smile with your heart,
laugh with your eyes.
Let love be irresistible!

DAY 110

God, what would you have of me today?

Today I would have
what I would have every day:
    your complete attention.

I would have your mind, heart, and soul
attuned to me.
I would have our oneness.
I would have my thoughts be yours,
    and yours, mine.

Your reactions and responses
will then be graced with my divine essence,
allowing spirit to flow
    in a way that ushers in blessing.

Listen to your heart.
Trust your instincts and intuition.
    Do not second-guess yourself.

Lift up this day as an offering.
Live it as a sacrament.
    Give me the outpourings of your soul.

EVENING REFLECTION

Today I spent most of my working day at the piano composing. With the guidance as a reminder, I was more conscious of staying attuned to Spirit during the day's activities, which included dealing with the technical aspects of recording. I worked with my intuition and incorporated ideas without second-guessing them. I trusted my thoughts and inclinations to be part of my oneness with God.

The result was that I composed a difficult piece of music very quickly. The most beautiful part of the process was thinking of my work as sacrament and offering. That greatly affected the way I approached the day, the work, and the results. I poured out my soul as an offering, and when I played the music back I did it as sacrament.

It was a beautiful process that I can apply to any endeavour.

How did you live into the guidance today?

DAY 111

God, what would you have me say, do, or be like today?

Be quiet...
but be present.
Receive others calmly and patiently.
Be aware of your capacity to hold others
in love and care,
    and do so.
Move with grace,
and let your words show understanding.
    Be a soft place to land today.
Stay divinely rooted
and extend love without conditions.
    Let go of your agenda.
Be present for others.
When you do this,
    you will feel my smile.

EVENING REFLECTION

Someone I know needed a good friend today. I became that soft place to land. They were able to tell me what they were holding, and, as they did so, I could sense my capacity to hold another in love and care as I let go of what I wanted to get done today.

It can be a challenge to stop, pull back, and make room for others. We all need to be heard, but who will do it?

Today I let go of my plans and walked with another. It led to a beautiful day. I went to new places, saw different scenery, and enjoyed wonderful conversation. And yes, I felt Divinity's smile in my soul.

How did this guidance affect you today?

DAY 112

God, what would you have me say and do today?

Be especially helpful today.

Go out of your way to be of service to those who
need help.
Have genuine interest in the challenges another is
facing today.
Ask how you may be of help.

The practice of extending yourself
in service to others
will reveal how your own needs are still met.

Be patient with yourself and let go of resistance.
Smile and be as cheerful as you can be.
Be truly glad to help whoever is sent your way.

To bless another by adding your love, care, and
service to their day
is to be my ambassador
and serve as an angel on earth.

Will you be that today?
All day?

EVENING REFLECTION

We live in a world where it seems everyone is going
100 miles per hour all the time. With this pace of life,
who has time to take time for others? Today's guidance helped me to slow down and look around. It
made me pause and look at what others might be
challenged with.

Not much happened today, and by the time 10:00
p.m. came around I saw that my wife was preparing
for bed. She was going on a cross-country airplane
flight the next morning and wanted to get a good
night's rest. As I know her bedtime ritual, I took a
glass of water up to her. She said, "Thank you, God!"
She was so tired she hadn't wanted to go downstairs
to get some water, and she thanked me for being
thoughtful.

I thought of the last lines of the guidance, about
how blessing another makes you an ambassador of a
loving God. My wife's appreciation for this small act
affirmed the power of love, care, and service. And it
demonstrated to me that even a small act of kindness
can be powerfully received and appreciated.

And since this occurred around 10:00 p.m., I am reminded that the challenge was to be helpful all day.
And all day means all day. I could have called it quits
before 10:00 p.m., but seeing it through yielded a
blessing for another, and husband points for me!

How did you do?

DAY 113

God, what would you have me say and do today?

Be the silence within silence.
    Quiet your being.

Allow peace to prevail, no matter what transpires.
Remember, outside of loving me with all your being,
    having unconditional love for all people,
        and reverencing all creation,
            few things are as important
as you want them to be
or think they are.

And it came to pass (and it did not stay)
is true of most things.

Being at peace is more important than
getting your own way, proving your power,
or asserting your authority. Life goes on,
no matter what.
The question is, does peace go on with you?
Remember the phrase, *Let go and let God.*

You can avoid stress by remembering this
blessing:
Let peace – your peace – have the day.

Take it easy on life today.
You are truly most alive when you can rest in
peace.

DAY 114

God, what would you have me say, do, or be like
today?

Be sure of my presence.
Walk in the light of my love and that of your own
enlightenment.

    Speak as one who knows security
is rooted in divinity.

Let that divinity glow through your every fibre
and pore.
How?
    By letting your light shine.

How to do that?
    Speak with love, and appreciate
and care for others.
    Relax and be present wherever you are.
Know you are where you are supposed to be.

    And know with certainty:
I am with you...
...always.

DAY 115

God, what would you have me say, do, or be like today?

Be quiet and strong like a mountain.
Speak with my voice,
because you are divine.
Listen closely to me so you may speak clearly.
Stay conscious of divine wisdom.
Its guidance is sure and its usefulness certain.
It offers life-giving love and healing.
Forgiveness becomes effortless, and doubts non-existent.

Work to stay conscious all day.
This is a powerful practice that will have
amazing blessings for you.
Can you – will you –
        do this today?

EVENING REFLECTION

I am noticing that every guidance roots itself in qualities that lend themselves to the unfolding events of my day. The guidance alerts me to when patience, or listening, or being soft, etc., would be particularly useful in the moment. It seems to do so without my calling it up. It is as if my spiritual instincts know what is needed.

How have you noticed yourself growing? What qualities in you are becoming stronger? More developed? What aspects of your growth are surprising you? What are you enjoying about your personal growth and progress?

DAY 116

God, what would you have me say, do, or be like today?

        Today, be moist of heart.
        Stay wet with love's dew.
Let your heart be drenched by the divine rains
        of appreciation and gratitude.

Bathe in the grace of my love and care.

        Swim with me all day.
        As you talk and move, enjoy knowing
that you live, move, and have your being
        through and because of my mighty spirit.

Receive with joy all that comes your way.

All.

        Enjoy the blessings that may be hidden inside
        the nuances of the day.
Stay moist.
        Let your heart be filled with joy.

You will connect beautifully with me
        and with all of life today.
        Let it be.

DAY 117

God, what would you have me say and do today?

Let your family and friends know
how thankful you are for them.
    Let them hear your words
        of gratitude and appreciation.

Demonstrate your thankfulness.
Smile and look into their eyes with gladness.
    Let your heart extend love.

Give a small gift to someone you appreciate,
    just because.
Call someone just to pass on a quick message of
gratitude.
    Listen today with the ears of your heart.

Ask questions that touch the soul.

You will bless those you reach out to,
    and feel the blessing come back to you.

Are you ready?
Have fun being a blessing-giver today.

EVENING REFLECTION

Words cannot capture the joy I witnessed as I thanked people for their efforts and for being who they are. The affirmations and appreciations came back to me tenfold in ways that are difficult to describe in words. It is sort of like trying to explain how virtue is its own reward. It must be experienced.

When I matched a compliment or appreciation with a kind look, a smile, or an added question, I saw the difference it made to the other person. And it just plain felt good to give out a...well, blessing. I blessed family members, friends, and acquaintances. I blessed people who let me in as I merged into traffic.

Today's guidance encouraged me to extend myself toward others, and that helped make the day fun to live. Not only did I see other people rise a little higher in their inner being as they received my heartfelt compliments and appreciation, but I felt my own soul rise and expand. It is hard to describe, but it is that feeling you get when you know you are being a better person, perhaps even a beautiful person, a person who is growing spiritually.

How did you do with this guidance?

DAY 118

God, what would you have me say, do, or be like today?

Rest in the knowledge that
    I work all things for good.

As you live into this truth,
be aware my timetable
    is not like that of the everyday world.

Resting in my timing means trusting that I am
for you
and always working for your highest good,
    even if it doesn't look that way.

If you can trust this...
it renders all things blessed for those who let go
    and invite my spirit in.

Work today, with all your heart, mind, and soul.
Then, let it be.
    I am in control.

EVENING REFLECTION

Letting go and letting God is freeing. Many people want to have complete control of everything they do and get stressed when things do not happen as they want. Reminding myself that God works all things for good allowed me to relax today, even as I worked hard. I am not responsible for the results of my life's work, but I am responsible to do the work. Then I must let go. It is comforting to know I am not doing my life all by myself. I know I am part of a picture too big for me to manipulate. I am reminded of the proverb that urges us to work as if it all depends on us and pray as if it all depends on God.

How did you do today? Were you able to rest your soul in the midst of the busyness of your day?

DAY 119

God, what would you have me say and do today?

Do what is helpful and supportive.
Say what is encouraging and enlivening.

Respond with genuine feeling rooted
in the love of all things.

Support your co-workers
and let them know you are grateful
to be working with them.

Relax, be calm,
and trust that all things are worked for the good.

Let your loved ones hear of your love for them
today.

Move your own needs aside
and be present for those who cross your path
today.

EVENING REFLECTION

To move aside our own agenda in order to be present for others is a great spiritual exercise. It lets us know that we are able to help others and still accomplish our own goals. It is also a beautiful reminder that we are here for each other, not just for ourselves. And during the process of expanding our vision and enlarging our purview to make room for others, we grow as human beings.

Now, making room does not necessarily mean moving aside to the extent that we let someone take advantage of our kindness. It doesn't mean ignoring an important deadline. It means being big enough of heart to take the time and make the space to help others. Each time we do this it adds to our own beauty and makes creation more glorious.

DAY 120

God, what would you have me be like today?

Be a saint...
    selfless, and wholly committed to serving
God.

Be willing to go the extra mile for someone in
need,
    sacrificing your own agenda to serve
another.

Listen for divine guidance.
    Be fairly quiet. That will help you hear.

Make your work
    a sacred offering.

Be humble with everyone you meet today.

Let love shine through your eyes.
Let love's dew drench your words.
Let your heart be light.

Give your burdens to me today.

Be a servant saint today.

EVENING REFLECTION

I was forced to think about what being a saint meant to me when I received this guidance. My religious upbringing was an influence. So was the popular notion that a saint is someone who goes beyond the call of duty to help another. We would probably never call someone who deliberately causes harm a saint.

I see a saint as being someone who consciously and consistently strives to live a spiritual life at a high level. So it was a deep privilege to be asked by God to act as a saint and be of service to God and to others.

Just when I thought I had reached some satisfaction with my sainthood effort today, I had a conversation where the devil in me suddenly reared its ugliness. Someone pushed a button and the saint in me came tumbling down. Arrgh! It just goes to show you that as good as God is at being God, there will always be excellent adversaries to our saintliness.

Oh well, I can try again tomorrow. For the rest of the night the keywords are *forgive* and *forget*.

How'd you do?

DAY 121

God, what would you have of me today?

I want you to practice being an understanding
person today.
    Place yourself in someone else's shoes
    as best you can.

When you set aside differences you humble
yourself.
    You then have a greater capacity to avoid
defensiveness
    and are more able to maintain peace.

Of course, there are adversaries of peace;
expect resistance. To succeed, you must
commit to understanding.

Commitment to understanding
opens the door to grace.
As you extend your heart of love
– no enemies or personal affronts to defend
against –
you will feel the power of peace.

    Can you be this strong?
Yes, you can.

Will you?

I found that to live into this guidance I had to meditate on it constantly. Ego is a tricky part of our human nature. It wants to be like God and will pull out
all kinds of tricks to thwart being pushed aside. But
keeping this guidance to the forefront of my consciousness ushered me into a space that made the
effort of controlling my ego easier. The space had the
feeling of a lush, green meadow surrounded by beautiful, towering mountains. There was a stream flowing through it. And everything I needed was there.

Still, it took commitment to live out today's guidance. (I like to say that "power" can be spelled c-o-
m-m-i-t-m-e-n-t.) As the day went on it became easier
and easier to extend myself into the souls of others.
I was not so much an "I" as I was "awareness." Awareness looking and observing. And this awareness felt
divine. I was not so much a body as "is-ness." In this
space there was no need of my ego and its influence.
Spiritual masters can remain in this space for extended
periods. But to have glimpsed it was beautiful.

How was your experience today? Were you able to be
understanding and push your ego into the background?

DAY 122

God, what would you have me do today?

Be soft
    and loving.

Be supportive
    and understanding.

Keep your voice low
    and sweet.

Listen with sensitivity,
    and empathy.

Be present
    without being demonstrative.

Let softness direct all you do today.

DAY 123

God, what would you have me say, do, or be like today?

Be a source of peace.
    Be in a state of peace.
        Walk in communion with peace.
            Give everything to me today.

Be peace. Be at peace. Be peaceful.
    Let go of all worries today.
        Give your concerns to me.

        Breathe out and just let them go.

    Move through the day with faith,
and trust the unfolding.

Peace be with you...
    And it is.
Will you receive it?

DAY 124

God, what would you have me say, do, or be like today?

Be kind
    no matter what.
Practice being kind
    in all situations.
Remember that the power in kindness
is greater than the strength of force.

Events are temporary.
I supply all you need.
Know that you will get through present hardship
with grace and beauty.
Grace and beauty are available if you want them.

Be joyful, knowing you are loved.

Be helpful and loving.
Let go of any anger that challenges peace.
Do not let ego Edge God Out.

    Be like a peaceful meadow
      with the warm sun shining upon it.
    Invite and welcome all creation.
  Be kind to all beings today.
All day.

DAY 125

God, what would you have me say and do today?

Speak with faith and hope.
Demonstrate your belief
in the goodness of life
and your trust in me.
Know you are held
    in love and divine grace.
Gratefully receive the day's blessings.
Let my love and care for you melt your doubts.
Let your light shine for others.
My grace is yours today.
    But not just today.
Always.
Live today knowing you are blessed.

Be well, and be blessed.

DAY 126

God, what would you have of me today?

     I would have your sensitivity.
Be conscious of what others are feeling and
holding.
     Respond in assuring and understanding
     ways.
Support others and hold them in love.

Sink into the background to make room
     for others to be first.

     Ground yourself in divinity.
     Drink from its ever-gushing fountain,
and receive all that you need to perform this
service.

Live for others today.

EVENING REFLECTION

The focus on the subtle qualities that make us beautiful people in our everyday lives is what makes each
guidance so powerful. Breaking down the phrase, "be
a good person" to the particular fine qualities needed
to "be a good person" helps us bring to consciousness the subtler aspects of ourselves that we want to
develop.

Sensitivity to others is one such beautiful quality. It
helps us to get outside ourselves. It reminds us to
place ourselves in the shoes of another and then respond compassionately. And that makes every one of
us a more beautiful human being. And not just for
this day, but for every day we live out this quality.

So how did you do with the guidance today? In what
specific ways were you sensitive?

DAY 127

God, what would you have of me today?

I would have your concentration
     and creativity.

This requires an open spirit
     attuned to me.

It means that you must discern
     when your ego gets in the way.

It means you must trust my spirit
     to move and guide you.

You are an instrument of my divinity,
     full of my grace.

Give yourself back to me
     and let me sound
          through you.

And through this divine collaboration
     blessings will come,
          power for life will emerge,
               inspiration will shine forth.

Yes, today I would have your concentration
and creativity.

Are you willing?
Are you ready?

EVENING REFLECTION

Today was a day of deep listening, watching, and
sensing. I sketched out a new song in my recording
studio. I was perhaps hyper-aware of my own ego
wanting to make the song rather than me allowing
God to create the song through me. I'd been down
this road before and reminded myself not to edge
God out even as I sought to create a song about the
Divine.

So today I was constantly letting go and letting flow.
Letting go of my ego and letting flow the Holy Spirit.
When it happens, it allows an amazing creative experience that is a collaboration of mind and soul,
spirit and divinity, skill and inspiration. In a word,
beautiful.

What are you birthing in your creative life?

DAY 128

God, what would you have me say and do today?

Celebrate!

Celebrate all that I have given you:
    your innate talents,
    your friends and family,
    your opportunities to work and play.

This celebration has nothing to do with the
achievements thought won by you alone.

    That is ego.

I want you to celebrate the blessings
hard won with effort and hope
or received as unmerited grace.

    You grow through both hardship and ease.
    Celebrate it all as it has all
    contributed to who you are now.

How to celebrate?

A thank you is enough.
Conscious acknowledgement will lead you into
moments of creative celebration.

    Shout, smile, dance, write a song
    or a poem, walk in nature,
    or light a candle and let it burn all day.

There are no limits to celebration.
    What will you do?

EVENING REFLECTION

I spent most of my time today recording in my studio, conscious of the joy of creating music. My celebrations included pushing buttons and turning knobs, moving to the music's rhythms, and joyfully playing different instrument sounds. Even while concentrating, I kept my heart open to receive inspiration's breath.

No one saw me. It was between God and me. I experienced a flow that allowed me to get a lot done quickly. After this all-day session, I celebrated by enjoying a beautiful dinner with my family – a dinner that I had prepared. And to the whole day, in final celebration, I said, "Thank you."

How did you celebrate today?

DAY 129

God, what would you have me say and do today?

Today, go deeper...
See past the surface.
See the beauty inherent in all things.

> Feel my love
> and see all creation
> with love.

Play joyfully.
Let joy give you energy.
Sing your soul in all you do today.
Nourish your spirit.
You are exactly where you are supposed to be.

> Relax.
> Be at ease.
> Work with purpose.
> Eat with appreciation.
> Rest with gratitude.

Will you do this today?
All of it?

DAY 130

God, what would you have me say, do, or be like today? What would you have of me?

Today, give me your trust completely.

Believe I have all matters in my care,
> and that all is working for your good.
Be faithful and confident
> and have no doubts.
> > Move and act with sureness.
> > Ask for wisdom.
Be like a tree standing strong in the wind.
Be firmly rooted in divinity,
> no matter how hard the winds blow
> or in which direction.
Today, like every day,
you are held within my divine energies.
> > Trust.
> > Trust.

EVENING REFLECTION

It is always amazing (if not surprising anymore) that the guidance brings with it a seemingly uncanny knack for knowing what is coming. About halfway through my day, my wife brought up an issue pertaining to a new website we had created. We had wanted a specific effect on the new site, but it didn't happen that way – and we had just sent out an announcement inviting people to visit the new site.

I brought out my daily guidance and read it. My wife had already stated, "Well, maybe God has other plans, and this is what is supposed to happen." We were both reminded that trust is a great peacemaker when things don't go as planned. We eventually got the intended look, but in the meantime we just trusted God to work it out and held to the belief that whoever was supposed to see the flaw would somehow benefit from it – probably in some way we would never hear or know about.

How is your trust in God these days?

DAY 131

God, what would you have me say and do today?

Be a refuge,
    a haven,
for someone who needs support and care.
With presence and softly spoken compassion
    say what is loving and reassuring.
Be a pillar of strength
    for someone today.
You need only be ready.
  Root yourself in my divine strength.
    Believe that all is well
      even when times are tough.
      Be grateful for the opportunity
    to live and have your being.
  Carry appreciation into all
you do and say.
Appreciation helps
create
  the space
    for you
      to be
        a
          place
            of
              quiet
                refuge.

EVENING REFLECTION

Sometimes the guidance seems irrelevant to my actual circumstances. And then something happens to make it *very* relevant!

Today I went to visit a friend – to drop by for a few minutes. A few minutes turned into two hours. My friend needed a place of quiet refuge and someone to listen. Hence I also needed to be quiet; to be a soft spot and a safe place to vent. I was in a position to become a refuge.

To be a place of quiet refuge means to support and not judge. It means to listen and love unconditionally without giving advice, warnings, or suggestions. It means being with a person and receiving their being – as they are – with understanding and compassion.

How did this guidance unfold in your day?

DAY 132

God, what would you have me say and do today?

Be joyful.
Awaken to the blessings of your life.
Let them infiltrate your soul and
all your endeavours today.

Let your actions show your appreciation
for all the good you have received.

Be at peace
    and know there is more to come.

Allow the refreshing waters of your joy
    to overflow,
that they may wash over others today.

You do not need to be boisterous.
Simply hold joy in your being.
That is enough.
It will shine through.

Live this day
    in joy.

EVENING REFLECTION

My wife and I went hiking today. As we took in the beauty of our natural surroundings, we made plans for our creative lives. We reviewed our challenges, as individuals and as a couple, and assessed where we might point ourselves.

After we offered the challenges, Jeannine suggested that we also offer our joys! At this point I remembered the day's guidance hidden in my pocket and laughed. Jeannine asked me why I was chuckling, so I read her the guidance. She responded, "Well, we must be on the right track."

It is always a wonderful gift to see the synchronicity of life and guidance. The metaphor we were experiencing was powerful. Here we were climbing a mountain – facing a challenge head on – and as arduous as it was, there was so much to enjoy in the midst of it (and even because of it)!

Where do you find joy?

DAY 133

God, what would you have me be like today?

Be calm beauty...
like a quiet morning with the sun highlighting
the brilliant colours in an alpine meadow.

Be conscious that your being
is enveloped by the luscious glory of holiness.

Let divine energy permeate you
and make you living light – beautiful and holy.

Let this image inform your words and
mannerisms.

Let the light within shine comfortably on
your day
and, through your actions, touch all with its
loving warmth.

This is a powerful and beautiful image to live
into today.

Will you do it?

Will you hold on to it?

DAY 134

God, what would you have me be like today?

Be responsive.

> Be attentive to me.
> Be awake to my leanings.

Move with me.
Surrender to my spirit moment by moment.

Follow my guidance and watch,
with awed enthusiasm, how smoothly the
day unfolds no matter what the challenges.

> Let peace flow into you and from you.
> Let unconditional love guide your words.
> Let compassion influence your actions.
> Let joy sing in your soul.
> Let holy light shine through your eyes.

Remind yourself
of the priceless gift of your life
and respond with humble appreciation and
willingness.

Give this day to me – starting now.

DAY 135

God, what would you have of me? Direct my steps today.

A prayer for the day.

Bring words to my heart and mind that are of your will.
Move my ego out of the way
that I may rest in your peace and kindness,
without defensiveness.
May I be a loving neighbour to everyone I meet today.
May gentleness and a soft spirit flow from me.
May I be grateful for the blessings in my life
and may I let your healing light and energy shine through me.
May I see beauty in all creation.
May I hold it all as sacred.
Guide me today, God, with your sure hand.
Breathe into me, that I may breathe love into all I am.
Thank you.

MORNING REFLECTION

This morning's question seemed to call for something different. I quieted myself and felt a prayer coming through. I could feel that it was a sort of summation of guidance so far, formed as a prayer request. And so I leave it. Even the Divine can give us prayers to say to the Divine. It is all one.

EVENING REFLECTION

I read this prayer many times today. It was especially helpful when I sensed I was drifting away from staying God-conscious. It helped me to bring my attention back to Divinity and reconnect with my deeper, higher self...again.

How did it serve you?

DAY 136

God, what would you have me say and do today?

Whatever you say and do,
remember that it all begins with me.
     Put the first word of your question
     together with the last word
and you get a powerful mantra:
     God today.

   Know all is in God,
       and those who live in love for the earth
           and all its inhabitants
       will be well
   always.
Know that my goodness and grace
always surrounds you,
swirls in and through you...

Live today in celebration of all things
that have brought you
joy and life.

DAY 137

God, what would you have me be like today?

Be open to learning.
Be slow to defend yourself.
Be quick to forgive.
Accept your imperfections.
Relax and know it is okay
to fail, even repeatedly.
You are divinely loved and known.
You are an awesome creation, held in great
esteem.
Your journey is a sacred one.
Your lessons are yours alone to learn.
Love all your experiences, even those hardest
to take,
for I am with you.
Accept my love...
            for there
                    is peace.

DAY 138

God, what would you have me say and do today?

Breathe consciously.
Feel your inhalation as life breath.
            All is well.

Breathe out gratitude, humility, and joy,
knowing that you do not carry your burdens
alone.
            All you face, you do not face alone.

Breathe out your hurts and challenges.
Breathe them out as an offering to me.
Receive grace and love by being willing.
            Let your heart receive peace.
Let your pain be pain but keep breathing deeply.
Keep making the divine exchange
of my peace for your pain.

Breathe...
Move your body to
help loosen the hold stress has on you.
Breathe, give thanks, and let me love you.

DAY 139

God, what would you have me say and do today?

Be unexpectedly kind.

Rest assured that your life is being used
for divine purposes.

Everyone you encounter is divine, as are you.
Your own divinity will
meet and excite the divinity in others
if you are present with it.

Don't push hard today. Let the work flow
smoothly through you. Enjoy each moment for
the gift it is.

Let the day's beauty open you
to the awe and wonder of creation.

Get stopped in your tracks by something.
Write a short melody or song,
compose a two-line poem,
dance a step or two, spin, jump…
Do something that reflects the awesomeness of
creation and your ability to create.

Are you willing to do these things today?

DAY 140

God, what would you have me say and do today?

Be a refreshing wind
blowing life into life.

Let your words soothe the souls
of those you encounter today.
           How?
Let what you say be of good heart.
           Your good heart.

Affirm others today.
Acknowledge their beauty.
Make them feel comfortable with who they are
by receiving them as they are.

Have fun with life today.

Infuse your challenges, worries, cares, and
burdens
with the lightness of your being.
Laugh at them, even if only for a moment.
Let the grace of humour lift you.

Let the divine wind uplift you
and swirl through you
as you become the breeze that blows
life into life today.

DAY 141

God, what would you have me say and do today?

Be aware of the gift of wisdom today.
Use the gift of wisdom to bring peace, healing,
and joy.
Think before responding or reacting.
Let your ego rest. Look for the lessons that are
yours to learn –
      and let them in.
Look for blessings hidden within your complaints.
Find joy within your unfulfilled wishes.
Be thankful for what you have.
Count your blessings and laugh at your follies
today.
  Be grateful you are alive.
    Be still...and know that
      you
        are
          blessed.

DAY 142

God, what would you have me say and do today?

Exercise patience
with yourself and those around you.
All are doing their best in every moment.

So are you.

Your blessings are too many to count.
To realize this is to truly acknowledge
divine love and grace.

Enjoy your accomplishments.
Rest your soul at some point today and reflect on
your material and spiritual achievements.

Sit quietly or go for a walk;
stop and appreciate who you are,
how far you have come,
and how you have grown.

Acknowledge the grace that has come your way.

Be humbled.
Humility connects you to compassion,
and compassion to patience.

Patience is a virtue.
It is one of the gems of spiritual maturity.
So today, exercise patience unconditionally,
and include yourself.

EVENING REFLECTION

The apparently simple guidance to be patient pro-
duced a day of seemingly limitless challenges to my
patience. As the guidance makes me more conscious
of my thoughts and actions, it also makes me more
conscious of the inherent challenges. It is as if there
is an equal and opposite force I must meet, match,
and triumph over in order to move onward in my commitment to spiritual growth and maturity.

At least that was my experience today.

What was yours?

DAY 143

God, what would you have me say and do today?

Take it easy.
Do not force any words or actions.
Do and say only what is heartfelt.
Wait for your heart
to let you know what to say and do.

> Live this way as a gift to yourself.
> Even if you are working a busy job,
> you can work with ease today.

Be thankful for the rest you are giving yourself.
Be calm. Breathe deeply. Walk slowly.
Tread the earth gently.
Receive its blessings
as you
> take it easy.

EVENING REFLECTION

Today I spoke with someone about his need to not take on so much. He needed a break, but he was finding it difficult to create one. I chuckled at the serendipity of the day's guidance, feeling that it might prove useful to this friend and colleague in this moment. I took it out of my pocket and read it to him. He told me that it helped him shift to a more hopeful attitude, especially the line, "Wait for your heart to know what to say and do."

If we follow our heart, we find it is a good leader.

DAY 144

God, what would you have me say and do today?

> Be thankful
> for everything today.
You can learn from every joy and every hardship.

Be thankful for heartbeat and breath,
beauty and love, friends and family.
Let your thankfulness be a sacred offering.
Give thanks throughout the day
for seemingly insignificant events,
as well as for the milestones along your journey.

Lift the day and all you do as a gift to me.
In joy and with gratitude, be a thankful person today.
> All right?

EVENING REFLECTION

It felt wonderful to personally thank people for being who they are and for being in my life. I felt tenderness, joy, warm-heartedness, and profound gratitude. I felt waves of divinity cascade through me when I built up another with genuine thanks. The phrase *Bless my soul* is one that captures the gist of what happens, for both.

Who do you need to thank?

DAY 145

God, what would you have me say and do today?

Be easygoing.
> Let the day flow as it will.
Even if there are things that must be done today,
do them with ease.

If things happen one way,
be fine with that.
If things happen another way,
be fine with that.

Let go of needing specific outcomes.
Be flexible.
> Bend to the shape of the day.

Enjoy ease.
> Let it bathe you in peacefulness.
Breathe easily and
release stress with each exhalation.

Be easygoing.

DAY 146

God, what would you have me say and do today?

> Be kind.
> Be a beautiful soul.

Take no offence to another's actions or words.

Whenever you feel your ego stirring, take a deep
breath and let go.
Allow your deep reserves of love and kindness
to rise within you.

Be willing to let things be as they are.
> Live the day
humbly and with gratitude.

Allow grace to flow through you
and permeate all you say and do.
Your spirit will know when you do so.
> You will feel the *Yes*.

If you can do this, many people will be blessed
by you today.

> Are you willing?

EVENING REFLECTION

Today's guidance initiated a change in my normal
demeanour. I became quieter than usual. In fact, two
people asked me if I was okay. (Not many see my
contemplative side!) Absolutely nothing was wrong,
and I greatly enjoyed carrying this quieter energy
into the busyness of a hectic day.

How did today's guidance affect you? How was it expressed in your day?

DAY 147

God, what would you have of me? What would you have me be like in the world today?

Be patient and understanding today.

You are a divine creation.
Use your divinity to love – no matter what challenges come today.

Let others be who they need to be and give them space.
Patience and understanding allow this.

Let inner turmoil find solace in your compassion for yourself.
Remember that life is not always easy.

Stay attuned to love today. That will make patience and understanding
easier to attain and maintain.

Know that all days, and all events, and all people have their own paths, as do you.
Exercise patience, breathe deeply,
and journey through today with eyes of love.

EVENING REFLECTION

I really loved this guidance! I think it helped me to live one of the most relaxed, patient days I have ever lived. That may sound a bit much, but it was my experience. I took in the words of the guidance in a way that allowed me to sit with people and not feel as though I had to get to the next thing on my schedule. I felt present and able to listen without inflicting my agenda or pace into the conversation. It let others be who they needed to be in the moment, and for moments and minutes and hours after that.

During phone conversations I felt like I was basking in the warmth of the other's soul. Even when the plumber arrived right in the middle of my workday I took the time to welcome him in. I did get back to my work, but I noticed I was much more at ease for having enjoyed a great exchange with a great soul.

It doesn't take extra time to be patient. I know that may sound like an oxymoron, but that is my experience.

Just as my day was heading into evening, a young family member requested his favourite fast food an hour before I had a music rehearsal. I was guest conductor for a church choir and this would be my first rehearsal with them. I was practicing for it and had planned to practice once more before the rehearsal, but figured I would have time to get the food and still do a bit of practice after that. Plus, I wanted to do the loving thing and be patient about my own agenda. So I committed to getting the food and rushed off to the restaurant – only to encounter the longest line I had ever seen there! *Seriously? Now?*

And then I marvelled: *How does the universe do this? Gives me a test just when I don't need it!* I felt Divinity chuckling in my direction: *You wanna grow? Well, here you go*! Patience and Understanding 101 – in a fast food restaurant. I debated whether to leave, or stay and trust Divinity to work things out, whatever that might look like. I decided to wait and trust – and then had to fight off the feeling of being a revved-up engine going nowhere. I kept breathing deeply and tried to stay calm and relaxed, even as time seemed to speed by. I finally got the food and rushed back home. As it turned out, I still had enough time to practice my music and be ready for the rehearsal. That is what I call grace.

What happened in your day?

DAY 148

God, what would you have of me? What would you want me to be like today?

Continue with patience and understanding today.
Stay relaxed, calm, and even-keeled.
Let the breaks of the day be what they are,
without complaint.

Breathe in peace...breathe out calm...
and continue to provide space for others to be
who they need to be.

Go about your day knowing that love
surrounds you, enfolds you,
and moves through you.
You are known, and you are blessed.

Hold this thought consciously and watch how
beautifully the day goes,
no matter what challenges you.

Bring all events into divinity, love, and grace
today.

DAY 149

God, what would you have me say and do today?

Say and do nothing without me.
Let me say and do through you.
　　　Pause...
just long enough for me to enter
before your ego responds for you.

Be peaceful no matter how you are tempted
not to be.
Be strong in love and humble of spirit.
Listen with compassion.
　　　Forgive any offence.
Live today knowing I am with you in
joy and pain.

I am – always – everywhere.

DAY 150

God, what would you have me say and do today?

Be easygoing.
    All is well.
Don't let others unsettle you.
    The problems
will be there
    tomorrow.

Recognize beauty
    and live in its glory,
all day.

People, places, events, situations,
    all have divine glory.
See it, acknowledge it, and
    be amazed.

DAY 151

God, what would you have me say and do today?

Whatever you say today, let it be gentle and calm.

Move with grace, and allow the divinity of
your whole being to shine.

Breathe deeply and slowly.
Let quiet be your inhale and serenity your exhale.

Let your eyes sparkle with joy
and let your smile be genuine.

Enjoy the unfolding of this day. Observe it with
wonder.

Find beauty in all things. Let beauty flood your
soul.

Watch others with interest.
Be present without getting in the way.

Be receptive to awe and open to surprise.

Let joy be your constant companion today.
Be light of spirit and merry of heart.

Will you do this today?

DAY 152

God, what would you have me say and do today?

Enjoy the beauty of nature.
Notice trees, grass, sky, flowers – whatever
is of the natural world.

Take time to feel the sun on your face,
the breeze on your cheek,
and the earth beneath your feet.

Let appreciation be your in-breath
and gratitude your out-breath.
     See with your heart –
       and marvel.

Let nature touch your soul,
for you too are nature.
Born of humanity
but divinely created.

DAY 153

God, what would you have me be like today?

Be my servant, ready and willing
to attend to the needs of others.

Be a blank page and allow me to compose the
melody and lyrics of the day.

Be obedient to my guidance in all you do and say.

Let me hold your hand
and lead you through this day.

Be my ready servant.

Are you willing to do this today?
Okay, here we go.

EVENING REFLECTION

Well, this was an interesting guidance for me. Because of it, I ended up grocery shopping, cooking dinner, and being a taxi driver (without pay). Perhaps those things would have happened anyway, but because of the guidance I was more conscious of responding to the needs of others.

However, in one instance I was not available when someone asked for my assistance. To make myself available would have meant cutting off the help I had already promised another. I could have double-booked myself in an effort to be super-helpful, but I also needed to be a good steward of my own time and energy.

Today reminded me that when someone reaches out and we are not in a position to help, we can engage our faith, hope, and trust that there may be another who is available.

God's universe is abundant, after all.

DAY 154

God, what would you have of me today?

I would have your complete attention.
    Focus on staying in touch with me
    in all you do, say, think, and feel.

I am not invasive; my spirit offers assistance.
    I do not overtake; I participate.
I dance with your thoughts, will, and feelings.
    I offer. I feed. I supply power.

Be attentive and let all things unfold
    without force or pressure.

Breathe deeply...receive *ruah*.
    Receive and respond,
    and watch a miracle unfold.

Are you ready?

EVENING REFLECTION

Today was challenging. I needed to begin creating a new music piece and woke up with a kernel of an idea in my head. I decided I should flesh it out, which demanded I learn some new recording skills. As I practiced the new skills, new ideas came, even as I realized other ideas would not work.

It was a slow, tediously plodding day of mundane work. But the guidance helped me to stay relaxed and not get frustrated with the slowness of it all. I breathed consciously and let the day unfold without trying to rush the creative process or speed up the learning curve.

By the end of the day I hadn't even come close to making headway with the project. But I had settled on a plan and learned new skills – and decided the project would be more fun done with a different, more organic approach. All the things the guidance expressed, I lived into today.

The miracle that unfolded was the grace God gave me. God's grace allowed me to let the day be just what it was. Grace allowed me to keep my peace, moment by moment, through a pretty mundane, nuts-and-bolts kind of day.

What was your miracle today?

DAY 155

God, what would you have me be like today?

Be like you at your best.

Now, to be at your best
you will need to *let go and let God*.
         And...keep doing it.
                  And keep doing it.
Also, one more thing.
         Do not be defensive.
Don't defend yourself, which goes back to –
         let go.
Inhale deeply and exhale slowly.
Be beautiful. You are, you know.
Stay close to me, your inner divinity and source
of joy.
Enjoy living this day! Let nothing throw you for a
loop.
Stay in the moment.
Keep calm; be steady.
Do not be surprised when you are tested.
Be ready. Stay in love.
Forgive yourself when you lose focus.
Forgive yourself and get back on track
         – your track –
of being the unique, beautiful creation you are.

Let your light shine brightly today.

DAY 156

God, what would you have me say and do today?

Say only what is joyful and enlivening.
         Leave the rest.

Smile,
appreciating the new day that has come to you.
Breathe,
knowing each breath is its own gift to you.

Let your kindness come through.
Offer peace, even just a kernel.
Offer what you can,
and kindness and peace will grow within you.
         How?
Kindness generates peace, and peace allows
kindness to grow without hesitation.

Today, resolve to be kind
in all circumstances,
and peace will be your reward.

With this peace, move through the day
satisfied that all is going as I would have it.
Smile with the joy of being alive.

DAY 157

God, what would you have me say and do today?

Be on your best behaviour today.
    Control yourself.
Do not let your mind think whatever it wants
to think.
Your thoughts influence your actions.
    Control your thinking.

Act and think
    from the heart of your divinity.
Stay connected to it.
Set your intention to be loving, caring, kind, and
gentle.
Then even your most spontaneous moments
will have the proper arc of expression.

The tone of your voice, your mannerisms, and
your overall demeanour will carry the light of
divinity and the grace of angels.

In all you do today, let challenge become
opportunity.
Receive any joy that comes your way
with gratitude.
Be not too shy to offer a compliment
or provide hope, joy, or healing.

None of this is difficult if you
    live the day
in the mighty and gentle grace of my spirit.
Set your compass and move in the direction of
    being your best today,
minute by minute, hour by hour,
    all day.

You can do it.

DAY 158

God, what would you have me say and do today?

Be kind.
Speak gently.

Notice something special in someone.
Appreciate it and tell that person if an
opportunity presents itself.

Wonder at the day.
Marvel at creation,
no matter the weather or your mood.

Tell yourself ten things you are grateful for.
Thank at least three people for something
they have contributed to your life.

Be conscious of how blessed you are, no matter
your present life circumstances.

Carry your inner light with humility and grace
and let it shine through your eyes, your words,
and all you do today.

Are you willing to do this?

DAY 159

God, what would you have me say and do today?

Say things that foster a sense of togetherness
with everyone you meet today,
from family members to strangers.

Treat everyone as your neighbour.
Transcend attitudes that are divisive.

Enjoy people and look upon them as beautiful
creations.

Dive into divine love and splash around.
Moisten your heart
so nothing dry and hard comes through your
words or actions.

Be joyous today!

DAY 160

God, what would you have me be like today?

Be godly.
Be unconditionally loving today,
    no matter what tests come along.

Just for today, practice this, no matter how
difficult.
Let go of any negative attitudes today.
    Take no offence today.

Know that I love and honour you.
Nothing can thwart this truth
or change this reality.
    You and your life are special.
So hold divinity within and be godly.

Be godly.

Relax and allow love to flow
from the core of your being
out through every pore
of your body.

You can do this.

DAY 161

God, what would you have me be today?

Be forgiving.
Be light. That is, take any offence lightly
so that the gentle spirit breezes
of compassion and forgiveness
may blow it away.

Make room today for a big heart.
Breathe open the door of understanding,
even if the only understanding is for you to
love and forgive without understanding.

Live to love today. Let it be a gentle, quiet
love that stands at the door
of your heart ready to step forward as a gift
of your spirit.

DAY 162

God, what would you have me say and do today?

See beauty...

in leaves shaking in the wind,
in handshakes, and milkshakes.

Hear beauty...

in the laughter of children at play;
in *I love you,* and *I'm sorry.*

Feel beauty...

in forgiveness and letting go,
in redemption, and second chances.

Today, soak in the beauty of life...
Watch for its subtle refusal to give up
on itself.

As you notice the ways
beauty makes itself known,
know that this is me saying,
    I am here.

Finally, today,
as you look deeply for beauty,
find your own, and let it shine.

EVENING REFLECTION

When you look for beauty you can find it even within those things you may regard as not-so-beautiful.

How is that?

It is because life itself is beautiful. The ugliness we humans cause to happen – as powerfully dark, tragic, and repulsive as it may be – is not what we ultimately choose to see and hold on to. Nor is it the reality we ever choose to live in permanently. And it has never triumphed over God's beauty. It cannot.

God is love, and love is beautiful. And we are made in love's image and likeness. Love is our true nature – our truest essence. Those who create ugliness are not yet willing or able to truly see or receive the beauty of life. True beauty touches the soul so deeply that we can discover the presence of God therein. When this happens, we are never the same. And we become people prone to both look for beauty and create it – in how we are and what we do.

What beauty did you see today?

DAY 163

God, what would you have me say, do, and be like today?

Be gentle with yourself.
Take it easy.
You can still work, and work hard,
but take things in your stride.

Do not overdo or try too hard.

Be comfortable in your life today.
Should a challenge or confrontation arise,
take a deep breath, relax, and accept it as part of life,
but do not give it any energy.

Let this day flow at its own speed.
Fill the moments of pause
with the awareness of the gifts of rest and silence.

DAY 164

God, what would you have me say, do, and be like today?

Speak with appreciation.
    Act with love and care.
Listen to others with attention.
Extend kindness and grace
    while expecting nothing in return.

Be grateful today for the journey you are on
    and for being alive.
        Be thankful.

Let joy quietly fill you today.
    Feel the immensity of the gift of your life,
        no matter the pressures and pains.
Be conscious of your place in the universe,
an honoured place of being
that only you can fill.

Give thanks for everything,
and for all you are.

For everything, and for all you are.

DAY 165

God, what would you have me say and do today?

Listen to my voice.
You will hear it deep inside yourself.
It will be quiet, but loud and clear.

Sense my presence.
It will be soft, but powerful and unmistakable.

Be conscious of my presence.
Today, there is something from me just for you.
Stay calm and ready.

Bring all stress and anxiousness to me,
and remember – there is never, ever failure
when you are in the grace of my love...
and you always are.

So be of good cheer – and know that I am God.

EVENING REFLECTION

I had a dream last night of me as the young man who pursued an acting career. I felt the drive and the excitement of my chosen profession. The dream morphed into dreamscapes of churches I had pastored, and classrooms I had taught in as a university lecturer. When I awoke, I realized I was in the midst of a life review. As I inch toward the completion of another decade of my life, my subconscious mind is getting a head start on ascertaining where I am and where I might go from here.

I decided I would spend the day in personal retreat if I could and was able to rearrange my schedule to do just that. I poured over my personal diaries and journals, looked through old pictures, and read sermons from years ago to see how my thinking had grown and changed. A poignant aspect of the review was sparked by the news that my favourite sports journalist had died of cancer at the age of 49. As I had lost my first wife to cancer and since, like the sportscaster, we had two kids, hearing about his death gave me pause. The list of his career accomplishments made me look at myself and my achievements again. It is always dangerous to compare, but I found myself taking stock of my ambitions and reliving where I had not achieved them.

I spotted a huge stack of sports magazines that I knew I would not read. I thought I should at least look through them before throwing them away, just in case something caught my eye. Well, something did. And what I read was so relevant to me on a personal level that I could hardly believe it. It was an article about short athletes. The shortest athlete they covered was five feet ten inches tall. I thought, *Wow, they think that is short*? I am five feet six inches tall. Still, it was inspiring to read about athletes who are considered short in stature playing sports populated by people a lot taller. The article focused on the perseverance and faith in themselves that the athletes needed in order to live out their dreams.

I got the message.

That led me to an article about a great (and tall) national champion college basketball player who then played in the NBA - and did not like it. His build and body type made it difficult for him to fit in to what the NBA, was looking for at the time. He ended up leaving the NBA and talked about the challenges of moving on when something is clearly not working.

I got the message.

I began praying that I might find new clarity in my own journey. I prayed that I might accept anew my build, my height, my skills, my accomplishments. I prayed that I might honour the still-powerful calling in the depths of my soul to inspire others through my writing. As I prayed my sister phoned from the other side of the country. She was with another woman and they had called to tell me of a new website they had started – one that was devoted to prayer! They wanted permission to use some of my material on the website. *And I was praying at the time?* That was some very tight synchronicity. Let's just say it was a divine appointment for all of us. I wanted prayer and here a whole network was being launched. I traded the rights to my material for their prayers. They prayed with me right on the phone.

Today I did listen – and I was listened to. And God sent two human angels my way, not to mention the messages that came through the magazine articles, the sad news, and a review of my own work.

It was a day where, though I was by myself, I was not alone. And I am ready to move forward, excited about the path ahead.

This is where one might shout for joy!

DAY 166

God, what would you have me say and do today?

You just did it.

You moved from doing something
without being awake to my presence,
to including me.

Include me in all you say and do today.
    Be aware of my spirit and presence
        at all times.

Move through this day gently.

Take time to read about someone else's journey.
This will provide insights into the journey of life
itself,
and will open you to compassion, empathy, and
humility.
These are rich gifts with which to bless yourself
and others.

Do not shy away from this task today.
Live the day with quiet joy and heightened
spiritual sensitivity.

EVENING REFLECTION

I began my morning the way many people do – I just started. I checked my email, made coffee, and began to think about the day's work. That is when I realized I had not thought about the One who had awakened me. I paused, thought, *thank you God*, and wondered what would come through the morning meditation. The initial message I heard was, "You just did it. You moved from doing something without being awake to my presence, to including me."

You have the rest of the guidance.

I lived the rest of this day in quiet joy and with a heightened sensitivity to life itself. I experienced pain as I took in the news of a horrendous crime half a world away. Still, I was glad that I could feel sadness, that I could at least pray, even though I had no real clue what to pray, except for the highest good in a terrible situation.

But I know prayer affects me, and I received some solace through caring about those who had lost their lives, and the families and friends who were left behind to deal with the tragedy.

God, to our eyes, may not always intervene or interfere, but God is always present – with love.

DAY 167

God, how would you have me be in the world today?

Be patient.
Let the day unfold at its own speed.
Let any anxiety melt into my
love and care for you.

Be kind,
generous and compassionate,
even of that which you
do not understand fully.

Be strong in faith
and let love carry the day.

Honour your weaknesses and shortcomings,
but do not live there.
Live in the blessings of your whole life –
and there are many, like the stars.

Can you do that?

DAY 168

God, what would you have me say and do today?

Be simple today.
Simplicity is like a breath of fresh air.

In the midst of the busy, complicated world,
be the smile that brightens someone's day.
Be the unexpected kind word.
Be the small act of generosity that gives hope.
Be the laugh that lightens a burden.

Simple acts of goodwill cut through darkness
and bring love.

So just for today, simply be simple.
What a blessing you will be in the world!

DAY 169

God, how would you have me grow today?

Be aware of wisdom
and allow it to guide you.

To be aware is to pay attention.
To follow is an act of will.
Mind over body, spirit over mind.

To live wisely is to live from your divine nature.
Wisdom is a higher consciousness,
   the holy essence
      of who you really are.

Lean into this guidance
and you will grow wiser.

Is this what you want?

DAY 170

God, where would you have me grow today?

Be aware of watching yourself.

Before you act or react,
connect with your awareness and
watch yourself.

Allow yourself the time and space to master your
actions, instead of letting your smaller, egoic self
be the boss of you.

Squelch anything that is not of love.
Dive below shallowness
      into the deeper waters of love and joy.

Take the initiative to exude peace,
which means you must be in peace.
Find it as you *let go and let God*.

DAY 171

God, where would you have me grow today?

Notice where you can be more loving.
Not in general,
but specifically.
Think about how you might extend
more love
to the people in your life.
Perhaps it is by phoning someone who is far away.
Perhaps it is by taking the time to listen deeply to someone.
Perhaps it is by dropping by to see someone who can't get out much.
Just look inside and commit
to the small acts of love
that come from the heart.
Grow
   into
      acts
        of
          love.

DAY 172

God, how would you have me be today?

Be like a deep river, silently flowing.
Let wisdom carry you through the day.
Be kind, accommodating, and tolerant.
Allow others to be where they are
without judging them.
Retain your inner joy and peace
no matter who or what challenges that.
Be of good cheer,
and take no offence.

Let wisdom carry you further along
your path of spiritual development today.

EVENING REFLECTION

There is something intrinsic to making a spiritual commitment that brings on testing. When I say I am going to be more loving, that's when the dog bites, so to speak. Sometimes I wonder just who is listening to my thoughts and mocking me!

Okay – now that I have that out of the way...

I wrote this at about 6:00 p.m....and it was *still* of great value. Why? We had surprise guests show up for a dinner event we had cancelled; then a freak accident sent a family member to the hospital. On top of that it seemed everybody was in a foul mood. And then! The weather suddenly turned windy and cold after being balmy! With all of this I'm supposed to accommodate others, retain my joy, and take no offence? Whew!

The guidance helped tremendously. It was as if the Divine knew what was coming and gave me a heads-up.

How did the guidance speak to your day?

DAY 173

Dear God, what would you have me say and do today?

> Take it easy
> on yourself and everyone else.
> Work within your limitations
> and be satisfied with your achievements.
> Have fun today.
> Breathe deeply and with joyful appreciation.
> Let this joy fill you.
> Enjoy the gifts of others
> and make the best of the day
> without fuss or fight.
> Take it easy.
> Have fun.
> Enjoy.

DAY 174

God, what would you have of me today?

> I want you to let go
> of your less than virtuous desires.
>
> Today, practice feeling at peace with yourself
> without needing anything from anyone.
>
> Don't seek approval, attention, or affirmation.
> You have it from me – always.
>
> Don't seek to be loved.
> You already are.
> Always
> and forever
> by me.

EVENING REFLECTION

Letting go. What a practice!

Letting go denies pride and ego their places as the bosses of our lives. They take over when someone pushes our buttons or critiques us, and we then react without thinking. But when we let go, we drop those defences. Letting go frees us from attachment to being right, good, powerful – or anything! Letting go allows us to be defenceless. We simply live every moment as the God-being we are. Nothing blocks our divinity. The kingdom of heaven is within us. And so we can be who we are, and allow others to be who they are. Other people's moods, attitudes, or behaviours will not get to us because we don't take anything personally. All are being who they are in the moment, including you and me.

Let go – and watch the peace that comes.

DAY 175

God, how would you have me grow today?

Let divine wisdom
focus your will
and its power.

Focus your intent on divine will and purpose
in every moment.
You will be blessed
with absolute peace
when you are doing my will.

If you lose this focus,
gently guide your will back to me
    and sense in your heart
        what is next...and next...and next.

Walking through the day attentive to my will
allows your personhood
to grow and mature.

DAY 176

God, what would you have me say and do today?

Show your love.
        Be gentle with your words.

Listen to others
        and extend to them your heart.

Give others, even strangers, the gift
        of your appreciation.

A smile, a nod, a kind act...offer these things
        with joy and thankfulness.

Enjoy extending the best parts of you
        and receiving the blessings that follow.

EVENING REFLECTION

This daily guidance encouraged me to show my love
and share it with strangers. It was particularly meaningful because it reminded me of the first sermon my
dad ever preached. I was six years old. He spoke of
the biblical injunction to "be not forgetful to enter-
tain strangers: for thereby some have entertained
angels unawares" (Hebrews 13:2 KJV). In theological
terms, an angel is a divine messenger. Any human
can be a divine messenger, even without their knowledge. So we may be sharing our love with a stranger-
angel.

Extending our love all the time is a challenge, but it
is a worthy goal. Loving is a way of being; it is a
lifestyle, and it is a choice. Make the choice, and the
power to fulfill it becomes accessible.

DAY 177

God, what would you have me say and do today?

Be gentle with yourself
and with others.

Allow nothing to ruffle you today
or jar you out of gentleness.
Rest in the truth that I hold everything.
This will help.

Keep to your plans
but leave room for divine change
as the day unfolds.

Yes, be gentle in the world,
and bless many souls...

EVENING REFLECTION

I did so well with this today. I noticed that being
gentle changed the way I moved and used my voice.
It even changed the quality of my visual energy –
how I looked upon the world. I so enjoyed the
awareness of being gentle with all those I came
into contact with.

Things were going so well until...well, until dinner
when I got into an awkward and slightly heated debate with a family member over something petty and
pointless. I lost my gentleness to my need to be right.

Coincidentally (or not!), prior to dinner I had taken
the guidance out of my pocket and put it away for
the day, thinking I had succeeded...and then wham!
Now I'm not saying the argument happened because
I didn't have the guidance on my person. But perhaps thinking that I had made it through the day as
a gentle man made me a little overconfident. I was
so disappointed in myself. Then I remembered to be
gentle with myself also.

I made peace with myself. Then I apologized to the
family member and identified what had pushed me
out of gentleness. We all had a good laugh at me.
Then I moved on – gently.

How did you fare with this today?

DAY 178

Dear God, how would you have me live into the day?

Let your unconditional love infiltrate every
circumstance.
In doing so, no one can wrong you.

Immerse the complications of the day in this love
and thwart any defensiveness,
anger, resentment, and passive-aggressiveness.

Move past...
    Grow...
        Mature...

Give it to me
and be at peace...

You are so loved...
so loved.

DAY 179

God, what would you have me say, do, or be like today?

Channel your energy through divine love.
Let love's wisdom and understanding guide your
reactions and responses.

Love with all your heart, soul, and spirit today.
Breathe in the love that always surrounds you.
Breathe out peace.

Patiently bear any frustrations
and disappointments
you experience today.

Forgive.
Let go.
        Move forward in joy and grace.
        Remember how blessed you are.
Smile.
Laugh.

Receive the many blessings of the day
with gratitude
and appreciation.

DAY 180

God, how would you have me grow today?

Begin by asking me
        your important question.

You already know the answer.
        Sense it within.

Yes, love is always the answer.
        It contains within itself everything you need
for spiritual development.

Grow by choosing love.

Know that love will guide you
to specific arenas and
areas of your development.

Remember to breathe as you feel into the margins
of your spiritual growth.

Breathe deeply
and let love support
your spiritual climb.

DAY 181

God, how would you have me be in the world today?

Be accommodating.
Be hospitable and welcoming.

Share readily and willingly.
Remember all I have is
    shared with you.
Be generous of heart today,
knowing that your selfless giving
adds blessing and joy to creation.
Today, you host life.
Bask in the joy of giving.
Whatever is asked of you, rejoice!

DAY 182

God, how would you have me be in the world today?

Be faithful and have confidence in me.
Remember my presence in your life.
Carry my love and peace within you.

Let your discontent have the day off.
Let acceptance and hope fill the recesses of angst
within you.

Live the day knowing I hold you close,
protect you, guide you, love you,
and cheer for you –
absolutely thrilled and excited
about who you are.

DAY 183

God, where would you have me grow today?

Let go of your grudges.
    Let go and move on.
Do your best to understand others.

Do not make a mountain out of a molehill.
Concentrate on the positives of the day –
there are always many.

What are you are grateful for?

Remember: *Keep letting go*.

Fill your heart with grace and goodwill...
and smile.

EVENING REFLECTION

Holding a grudge can make us feel important and powerful – and right. But holding on to a grudge takes an enormous amount of energy, and anything we give energy to grows larger in our minds. And each of us is responsible for what we hold in our minds.

Life is too short to hold on to perceived personal offences. We have seen over and over again that force doesn't change hearts. Love does. Love is the real power behind lasting change and transformation.

To hold a grudge may feel good, but it causes damage to the grudge-holder. Loving someone generates feelings of goodness in the most positive way. And ultimately, love is the only thing that heals the hurts of the world.

DAY 184

God, what would you have me say and do today?

I would have you own and accept that no one label defines you. You are always more than what is said about you.

Descriptions and labels are attempts to constrain your identity.
But stay unlimited, no matter what they say.
Stay close to your heart.
I place my will for you there.
You are of me,
and you are as unlimited
as I am.

Remember, a title may serve a fleeting need,
but *who* you are
is infinitely more important.

Be who you are,
no matter what label is attached.

DAY 185

God, how would you have me be in the world today?

Be a calm and cleansing mist
that permeates the air.

Speak words that refresh the soul.
Do what brings peace.

Let grace and love be present within you.
Let them manifest through your actions.

Let your heart be open, and
let the light within you shine forth like the rays
of the sun.

Bless all of life today with the strength and joy
of your love.

DAY 186

God, where would you have me grow today?

Listen closely to your heart.
Trust what it is telling you.

Be fearless in your faith
and follow where it takes you.

May every one of your actions fulfill
the deepest calls of your soul.

Work with gratitude; let grace
pave the way.

Watch for inspiration
in every moment.

Be content with your day
and give thanks.

EVENING REFLECTION

The soul knows what it needs to do.

After years of working in a musical group, I had come
to a fork in the road and decided it was time for me
to go another way. The difficulty was that after years
of working and creating together, bonds had formed,
a familial community had been created, and we loved
each other.

With the strength offered by the guidance today, I
was able to stay conscious of both my truth and my
love for every member. But I was also excited to know
that I knew it was time, and that my experience with
the band would be useful in the projects I was being
called to focus on.

DAY 187

God, how would you have me be in the world today?

Be pristine and fresh
   like a high mountain lake.
      Drink living water yourself
         then share the spirit of life.

Let grace surround you,
   flow through you,
      exude from you.

Kiss life today with your soul,
and feel how life kisses you back
with passion and unconditional love.

DAY 188

God, how would you have me be in the world today?

Be a love whisperer today.

Be light of carriage.
Be calm and peaceful.
Be graceful and thankful.

Act from the depths of your heart.
Touch others gently with your hands.
Let your eyes be a place of rest and comfort for those who look into them.

Let love whisper in your ear
      all day.

You are a divine
love whisperer today.

EVENING REFLECTION

Today was one of those days spent doing nitty-gritty, mundane work in my office. And I was tired from working late the night before. Still, I found I could use the guidance. I was conscious of the work looking into my eyes as I looked at screens and words. I whispered love to the work itself, which is my holy work, and which I do love.

When I did leave the house, it was to grocery shop. Walking the aisles and standing in line for the cashier were prime opportunities to whisper love. (I was too tired to do anything but whisper!) But then that is the synchronicity of guidance.

As I was leaving the parking lot, I passed a man holding up a sign asking for money. I had no cash, but I did look into his eyes, smile, and whisper love from the deepest part of my heart. His reaction was a priceless smile and nod of the head. We had a divine moment of sharing love and respect for each other.

How did you whisper love today?

DAY 189

God, what would you have me say, do, or be like today?

Be kind.
Be gentle.
Be loving.
Be a beautiful person today.

Stay attuned to your best qualities and let them manifest.

Let go of negativity or frustration whenever it shows itself.

Give every situation and conversation to me. It is not yours to handle. Not today.

Watch me being me
and rest your heart, mind, and soul, knowing I am holding it all.

Remember: it always was, and always will be thus...now and forevermore.

My car had needed a new windshield wiper blade for a while. But since it had not been raining, I let it go. Well, it rained the last two days and I have been trying to see through sheets of water – not very successfully.

Today I made time to get it fixed. I ended up going to a local business I had not been to before. I was upbeat and talkative and even admitted not knowing how to put a wiper blade on. The mechanic responded to my joy with his own, and we had a great time with each other.

After he had installed the new wiper blade, he held up the old one and said, "You bought this from me last week, right?" I replied, "No, I've had this one for a while now." He tried again. "YOU GOT THIS FROM ME LAST WEEK, DIDN'T YOU?" "Oh! Yes." "Okay then, I'll just send this bad one back." He went on to say that his second try was my last shot and that he would have charged me if I hadn't gotten his hint.

But I heard the blessing – and accepted it as such. If I had not taken in the guidance perhaps it would not have turned out that way. It wasn't about the $12.99 plus tax I would have paid. It was about the manager wanting to bless me for some reason. A blessing is a blessing, whether we deem it big or small. All blessing comes from the same source. And Source simply asks, "Are you willing to receive?"

DAY 190

God, how would you have me be in the world today? What would you have me say and do today?

Today, rest your soul.
   Enjoy who you are.

Be the person you are.
   Just be, and allow that to be enough.

Watch how your responses flow from your soul.
Listen to yourself speak.
Hear the beauty in your voice.
See yourself with your own eyes.

   Experience, as a gift to yourself, your own beauty, divinity, holiness, and uniqueness.

Today, enjoy the being I have made...as you.

EVENING REFLECTION

I attended a small function today where most of the people knew each other but didn't know me. Few made any attempt to reach out to me at all. I found myself concentrating on just being myself without the need for connection. I held on to the guidance and enjoyed consciously seeing out of my own eyes and watching my emotions and responses as I worked to remain in the beauty of my soul. I didn't strive to make the situation or setting different than what it was. I just tried to let my soul rest as I reminded myself to be who I am. This allowed me to remain comfortable in my own skin even in the uncomfortable setting.

Later I met with a friend who was worried about a new challenge. Someone had asked for his help editing a paper. He was not sure of his own skills in this area, even though he enjoyed editing and wanted to be a writer. I read today's guidance to him, affirming that he only need be himself and that would be enough. I reminded him that he had been asked to do this and that since the person asking must have some faith in his ability, he should too. I suggested that it would at least be an adventure in seeing where he was at as an editor. I pointed out that it was a gift to be given the opportunity, and it was a chance to be of help. Lastly, I communicated my hope that he would concentrate on enjoying being himself in the process. I am glad to say that when he left he felt more encouraged and was looking forward to the chance to be of service.

What did you experience through this guidance today?

DAY 191

God, how would you have me be in the world today?

Be content and at peace;
    want for nothing.
Perform the work of the day
with joy, gratitude, and appreciation.

Let inspiration find its way to you.
Read a book,
listen to a new song,
call someone who has been on your mind.

Love your life today
    and count your blessings.

DAY 192

God how would you have me be in the world today?

Trust my love for you.
Have faith in my ability to protect you.
Believe that nothing can come between us, even death.

Life in the body is temporary.
Today, share your fears with me
and rest in my peace.

Even when it seems the worst is happening,
    let my love give you courage.

My love is sure.
    I work all things for good.

EVENING REFLECTION

I had a medical procedure done this morning under anesthesia. I was told it was a routine procedure. But nothing is really routine when you know that the unexpected can and does happen. So, though I had no fear, I acknowledged life's unknowns. I then let go and surrendered to The One Who Holds All.

Did that help? YES. It may be one reason I went to sleep easily instead of fighting the drugs on some level. The reminder that life is more than the body is reassuring. To know that we can be in communion with Divinity whether under anesthesia or not – and that we are protected no matter what happens – is peace-giving.

DAY 193

God, what would you have me say, do, or be like today? What would you have of me?

Accept that you are human
and forgive yourself when your
perfectly imperfect human nature is revealed.

If you are able to see your errors
you are
        moving in the right direction.

Have the courage to make amends.
Take a moral inventory of yourself,
but let love rule your assessment.

And love does not judge.

Let divine love and grace wash over you
and rinse away guilt and shame.

        Yes, let them go...

You are human.
You are loved.
You are forgiven.
Love yourself.

DAY 194

God, how would you have me be of service today?

Today, do the work that your soul
calls you to do.

Move forward with the lifework you know you are
here for.

Remember that your work
benefits and blesses others.

Remember also that you have been blessed
by the efforts, work, and life callings of others.

Be confident that I will accomplish
my work through you.

Be excited for your chosen work.
Do it with grace and appreciation.
Infuse it with love and light,

and give it to the world.

DAY 195

God, how would you have me be in the world today?

Be accommodating.
Be helpful.
Support others today.

Make yourself available to assist others –
and do not think of it as sacrifice.
It's not sacrifice, it's service.

Do it in love.

Serve others in love,
and experience the beauty and blessing
of selfless giving.

Today, give of yourself
and bless the world.

DAY 196

God, how would you have me be in the world today?

Be a cheerful giver.
    Work on behalf of others,
        not just for your own benefit.

Remember how you are served by others.
Give in gratitude,
    as a way to bless the lives of others.

See your work as part of my work
to bless and love creation.

You, as a willing partner, have been given
    skills, talents, passions, and interests
to use for the benefit of all life.

Work humbly, with integrity and thankfulness.
Pray that you fulfill the tasks you have been
called to.
Pray in faith that you will serve the highest good.

Give, and enjoy the privilege.

DAY 197

God, what would you have me say and do today?
Where would you have me grow?

Grow your wisdom.

Pause and ask for guidance as you
encounter the situations of the day.

Remember that growth requires pushing through
boundaries into places you have not been.

Give me
your fears, hopes, and wishes.

Give over your human desires
and accept a more divine perspective.

Be willing, for this one day, to move
deeper into your heart,
deeper into your soul.

You will receive
gifts of love
far beyond earthly
satisfactions.

DAY 198

God, what would you have me say and do today?
How would you have me be in the world?

Be gracious.
Be gentle and kind.
Be a beautiful person today.
Let grace, love, and joy flow through your being.
Breathe in deeply
    and be aware of your divine nature.
Breathe out slowly and feel my presence.
Quiet yourself.
Bless the day with your smiles and laughter.
Be light in the world.

DAY 199

God, what would you have of me today?

Today, be quiet,
and concentrate on the work before you.

Today is a day to dive deeply
into your life work and sense its
import.

Even your simplest tasks are filled with
meaning and usefulness.

Do all things with care and integrity and
place them in my keeping.

Your life and work are not accidents.
You are part of a glorious tapestry of
divine works.

Work diligently today, and know the universe
is more beautiful because of it.

EVENING REFLECTION

Being quiet does not necessarily mean an absence of
communication. Silence lets that still small voice
speak, sometimes quite loudly!

I spend a lot of time alone when I write. But this
guidance asks me to acknowledge that I am not alone,
even if no other person is there.

Giving my work to God means not only acknowledging
God's presence but acknowledging that God actively
receives what I offer. Not to mention acknowledging
that my gifts come from God.

Giving over our work to God – letting it go – takes
commitment and trust. God entrusts us with our gifts
and talents, and we are privileged to entrust the fruits
of those gifts and talents to God.

Today, while holding in consciousness that even my
most mundane tasks are somehow more than I know,
I trusted that God would hold whatever I was doing
and do with it whatever serves the greatest good – a
good which is always based in love.

DAY 200

**God, how would you have me be in the world
today? What would you have me say and do?**

Be a warm, sunny, clear, calm day.
Include scenery that is beautiful, majestic,
and awe-inspiring.

So how do you become all these things?

Realize that they are holy reflections,
just as you are.

Carry the images within.
Hold them in your heart, mind, and imagination.
They will infiltrate
your words, actions, mood, and spirit.

Invite them in, give them space,
and let them play in you.

Breathe deeply
and shine brightly today.

DAY 201

God, how would you have me be in the world today? What would you have me say and do?

Bring joy
and efficacy to your lifework today.

Work quietly and diligently,
remembering that your work serves others.

Let your words show faith
in my movement in all things.

Be gentle with yourself today.
Appreciate your human traits
and honour your divinity.

You are living a great gift.
And you are a living, great gift.

Let this thought inform and transform
how you live into each moment today.

DAY 202

God, how would you have me be in the world today? Where would you have me grow? What would you have me say and do?

Be kind.

There are many tests along the spiritual path
that may awaken your shadows.
    Kindness shines a light on them.
When one of your shadows arises,
        pause...
        take a couple of deep breaths...
        and give yourself over to me.

    These tests are not accidental.
    They challenge your spiritual growth.
Your best intentions can rise on your behalf
if you move out of the way and let them.

Love with unflinching commitment.
And be kind.

DAY 203

God, how would you have me be in the world today?

Let the glory of creation
bathe you in its grace.

Let your eyes absorb beauty.
Let your ears hear the voices of creation –
the chirping of insects,
the rustling of leaves,
and the whistling of the wind.

Feel creation...
soft grass, solid rock,
silky water, coarse ground.

Let earth and sky, water and air
fill you with awe and wonder today.

You are privileged to be alive
in the midst of creation.

Let this truth bless you.
Hold it in your being and see how
it informs your attitudes.

Let creation's beauty
be lived by you today.

For you too are my beautiful creation.

EVENING REFLECTION

Today I saw the Grand Canyon. This breathtaking site quickly humbled me. However, I also saw people standing precariously on the edge of the cliff with their arms raised in triumph as someone took a picture.

Some of us raise our arms in victory because we are standing alongside such a display of creative power and grandeur. Others stand mesmerized by the beauty and size of the canyon. Then there are those who meditate or perform a ritual. It's as if we instinctively understand the absolute majesty of this creation and want to connect with its spiritual power in some way.

Today's guidance helped me not only to take in the immensity of the canyon in a highly conscious manner, but also to notice the small creatures – the chipmunk unafraid to come up to humans, the salamander crossing the sidewalk, the hawk floating on the updrafts.

There are many special places on our planet that express God's presence, power, and majesty. Though the Grand Canyon is one of those places, we do not have to travel physically to get to such a place. There is also a vast, deep, and wide space within us that is open to Divinity's beauty, majesty, power...and love. We can get there by way of prayer, meditation, or contemplation. We can get there by selfless service, or by doing any mundane task, such as peeling potatoes, with care and attention.

It is love that leads us to the grand places in ourselves. And we can go there anytime.

DAY 204

God, how would you have me be in the world today?

Be relaxed.
Don't rush anything or anyone.

Let everything have its own rhythm today.
Let your steps have a cadence that says you
have time to take your time.

Let your words flow with a smoothness that
allows you to savour conversation.

Let your touch linger just long enough to get past
surface niceties, whether
you are simply shaking hands or hugging.

See the day with your heart;
feel the sun with your soul.
Pause in the breeze and feel its caress.
Taste food with appreciation.

Experience life with your whole being
as you swim in the ocean of creation.
Relax, and let grace take you through the day.

EVENING REFLECTION

The universe knows just what you need and gives it
to you – even if you don't want it.

Today was a challenge. I was at the DMV. Yes! The
Department of Motor Vehicles. Being at the DMV is
often an exercise in imposed waiting. And there are
two choices. One is to be frustrated, while the other
is to...relax. I chose to relax and was thus ushered
into the wisdom and grace of the guidance. I found
myself walking to the beat of my own drummer, not
the tick of the watch. My own pace, my own cadence.
And I knew – again – *Oh, so this is my natural pace.*

I became more present. I had time to step outside –
and just stood. I felt the caresses of the wind and the
sun on my face and in my soul. I saw the day with my
heart. All this while waiting at the DMV! The mad-
ness of the mundane became a respite.

The beautifully painted sky at sunset made dinnertime
a sacred delight. It invited relaxation and slowing
down. I recognized many gifts, including food, family, love, and the grace that allowed me to wake up
this morning, live the day, and now see the unfolding
of night.

How did your day unfold with this guidance?

DAY 205

God, what would you have me say, do, or be like today? What would you have of me?

Live this day in peace and calm.
Speak words that are
light-filled and life-giving.

Receive my grace and let it
permeate your being.

Be a light on the earth today.
Immerse all you do in love.

Shine my light into any darkness.
Let the gifts of prayer, love, faith, and hope be
your aid.

Move through this day as an ambassador of the
Christ spirit,
carrying with you blessing and compassion,
love and forgiveness, peace and grace.

This is your calling, your birthright,
your inheritance as a divine being.

DAY 206

God, what would you have me say and do today?

Celebrate the astounding privilege of life today.
     How?
That is up to you.

To celebrate is to appreciate with joy and
to express that joy and appreciation.

It doesn't have to take much time,
but celebrate earnestly
so that the gratitude flows
from deep within.

You will get closer to the awe and wonder
of my precious gift to you –
     your life.

DAY 207

God, how would you have me be in the world today? Where would you have me grow?

Make time
to care for what you care about.

Attention is a powerful thing.
  It is a force of its own.
    Live this day attentive to the things
that are most important.

To whom do you need to express love? How?
What work is calling you?
What do you need to tell yourself
    about yourself?
Where do you need more balance?
How can you create that?

Today, take stock of what you love
    and the calling within you...
      and let balance be your aim.

When we pay attention to something, we tend to lean that way. We get what we focus on. Science has demonstrated that observing an experiment creates its own change to the experiment because of the power of attention placed on it.

When I am immersed in a project, I can neglect other things unintentionally, including people, my own body, or the care of my soul.

It is good to remind ourselves to pull back and water the plants, or give a loved one a hug, or go for a walk. When we do things that we consider mundane in the midst of what we consider to be important, we can reconnect to the importance of the simple acts. They can be the space that renews and nourishes us. They can refresh our inspiration even as we rest our brains. And they can connect us once again to what is most important.

DAY 208

God, what would you have me say and do today?

Today...relax.

Do what you must,
according to your responsibilities,
but relax.

Notice that life can be lived peacefully, restfully,
and calmly,
no matter the circumstance.

Your inner life is yours...

    breathe in peace,
      breathe out calm...
    breathe in calm,
      breathe out relax...

Speak and act from calm energy,
knowing that stress can be met with
the spiritual agency of
    peace...
      calm...
        relax.

Breathe them in, hold them in, live them out.
Be blessed with them today.

DAY 209

God, how would you have me be in the world today?

Be mild-mannered.
Breathe deeply
   and meet the world with hope.
Let hope fuel your thoughts, your words,
and all you do today.

Notice what is, and let it be.

Let hope shine on all your endeavours.

Let a vision of what could be
find inspiration and strength of heart in you.

Be mild with yourself and the world,
and live well today.

EVENING REFLECTION

I was met today with news that opened some childhood wounds – experiences that had revealed to me the worst of the human condition in ways I hadn't wanted to believe and could not control. The news triggered powerful and intense emotions, including anger and sadness. I stayed with them a good while, allowing them to just be. But then I had a choice to make: I could stay in that space or let in something that could usher in healing. I reminded myself that all I really have control of is myself – how I think, act, respond, and live in the world.

Today's guidance was a reminder that hope is a powerful and useful tool in life. It can keep us from drowning in sadness, wallowing in self-pity, or becoming cynical. Holding a vision of what might be can inspire a soul not to give up. Strength of heart lets us be willing to look at triumphs, however small, and claim them as signs of possibility.

Being mild-mannered in a world of drama is no easy task. Fierce feelings such as anger, resentment, jealously, envy, and hatred are easily and widely promoted and consumed through movies, television, video games, newspapers, magazines, and other media formats. Being mild-mannered is often considered to be boring and, in some social climates, even dangerous, although it actually is a powerful way to be.

Try it for yourself today. And if you already are mild-mannered...then carry on.

DAY 210

God, what would you have me say, do, or be like today?

Stay aware of the larger context.

You live in divinity.
You are a being of light and love.
Your words carry light from your heart,
and love from your soul.
Your actions have power to transform –
    a smile sent toward a stranger
    can change a life.
Breathe deeply,
and pause often
to reconnect with me.

Let the content of the day be
what it will be.

Let the context be love.

Immerse the day in
YOUR
love.

DAY 211

God, what would you have me be like in the world today?

Be confident in the work
I have given you.

Perform it diligently.
Finish it.
Bring it to fruition.

Let your doubts be gone.
Be done with them.

Remember that your sincere intention
to do good
serves humanity.

  Let this carry you.

Be inspired by my love for you.

Fulfill your calling
with gratitude and appreciation.

  Move forward today;
work out your sacred calling.

It is so easy to let doubt creep in when you are labouring over material that you hope to bring into the marketplace. The questions can be incessant: *Is it good*? *Am I good enough*? *Am I worthy*? The doubts can be debilitating: *There's too much competition. This is just a waste of time. I am an unknown.*

Today's guidance reminds us that doing what calls us is what is important. If we do not, we suffer inner turmoil, self-disappointment, and frustration. We can self-publish. We can make our own music and put it on the Web. It should not be about the money. It should not be about fame. It should be about answering the call in your soul. Whatever happens after that is a God thing.

Many years ago, I was invited to present to a very small gathering in a very small church in a very small town. I delivered a poem I had written and received a standing ovation. After the event a man stopped me, my wife, and my son on the sidewalk. He said to my son, who was about six years old at the time, "You know who your dad is? He's a wordsmith. One of our best." Then the man smiled and walked away. I said to my wife, "If that is so, why am I not performing in larger places, and why am I not well-known?" My wife simply said, "Perhaps God has placed you here because these people need to hear your words too."

Money is not the marker of success. And it won't make you happy if you are not doing the work you are called to do. Doing your life work and living your life purpose are better markers of success.

I like this axiom I learned not so long after that event:

Success is getting what you want.
Happiness is wanting what you get.

DAY 212

God, how would you have me grow today?

Stay close to my spirit
   for as long as you can.
Contemplate me as you engage in your day.
Consciously include my presence in all you do.

I will not get in your way
but I will infuse your thoughts, actions, speech,
and insights with divine grace and energy that
will inform and elevate your responses.
If you maintain your conscious contact with me
you will be able to hold on to me
when the world tempts you away.

Will you do this today?

EVENING REFLECTION

I am starting this response at 3:57 p.m. because I just experienced a small miracle and want to write it down while it is still fresh in my mind. I was printing out pages for this book in order to review them when I "felt" I should check to see if they were being printed okay. I was using a printing method that allowed me to print without first looking at the document, and I was unfamiliar with it. After paying attention to this "feeling," I went to the printer and looked at the last document printed.

It had an error in formatting.

I thought, *Whoa, I'm glad I caught that.* Then I looked at the documents printed before that one and none of them had the error. I thought that was amazing. Then I thought, *Well, I got lucky and caught it. I had better slow down and check the rest as I print them.* I printed the rest of the documents by opening them first, checking them, then printing. The difference in speed was negligible and it allowed for more efficiency. It turned out that none of the documents printed after the one with the error had the formatting error...

...ONLY THE ONE I SOMEHOW FELT THE NEED TO CHECK!

How did it happen that the only one to have the formatting error was the one I decided to check?

I don't know, except to say that my guardian angel, God's messenger, must have gotten through to me. And what was the point of that? you may ask. After all, I most likely would have found the mistake in my hard copy review. Well, I think the point was to let me know that the Divine was undeniably with me. I can't prove it was a divine communication, but I have learned that these *markers* are for me alone. (I call them markers because they "mark" God's presence in a more overt way.)

The daily guidance encouraged me to stay close to God today. I was conscious of my work being a co-creation with Divinity. I was in a quiet state of appreciation and gratitude, and I was aware of doing the work as a sacred service for anyone who might come to use this book. So one outcome was an encouraging moment propelling me forward in the creation of this book.

We all have had incidences when we don't follow an inner guidance and then regret that choice. But here was an occasion where I followed the spirit. I don't need to know whether it was God, an angel, or some other divine means that got through to me. What I can attest to is the divine communication that happened and the feeling it engendered within me. It was my own proof, once again, of God's ability to get through to me, guide me, and be with me.

All I could really say in that moment was, "Thank you." And that is all that needs to be said.

DAY 213

God, what would you have of me today?

I would have your time.

Dive in and stay with me all day.
You will notice that your choices
are tinged with my grace.

You will notice the sureness
of my spirit, and you can rest
knowing that your best efforts are both
blessing and blessed.

When you sense that you
have drifted from me, simply pause
and turn your thoughts toward me.

And time will stand still...
as you enter my eternal presence.

DAY 214

God, how may I be of service today?

Be aware of the greater good today.

Being aware of the greater good means
seeing beyond your likes and dislikes.
It means paying attention to me.
It means caring about
the happiness of others.

It asks for your wisdom and discernment.

Ultimately, it is about love.
It always is.

So today – love.

Love yourself,
and love each person with whom
you share the stage of life.

Loving adds blessing and glory
to the universe,
deepens your soul,
and widens your heart.

EVENING REFLECTION

A friend stopped by today. He needed a listening ear, although he said he was stopping by to pick up some money I was willing to lend. When he arrived, he said he needed 20 minutes of my time. Well, two and a half hours later – after an outpouring of deep sadness, heartache, and grief – we parted.

The greater good today was about being a listening ear and giving feedback. I was in the midst of my own work, but it was clear that this friend needed someone and had picked me. I had the time and space for him, but was I willing? I was smack in the middle of my workday and on a roll. But I remembered the guidance and trusted its intent and timing. I could give the time.

It was about love. It always is.

But after two and a half hours, I also felt the need to love myself by ending our time together. I felt I had given all I could give in terms of support and encouragement. As I was gently ending our time together, my friend said he did not want to leave. What he meant was that he wanted to stay in the bubble of the lovingkindness he was receiving. I felt guided to give him a blessing, and I let him know I would be here if needed. I reminded myself that part of supporting someone means knowing how to support yourself. My friend then told me that he had to leave anyway to get ready for an appointment.

I did call him a few hours later and he thanked me for my time. He said he felt much better and had been able to enjoy the rest of his day.

The *greater good* ended up being...just that.

DAY 215

God, how can I be more loving today?

Take care of yourself today.
Be aware of your actions
and whether they nourish you.
Find ways to enrich
what is not fulfilling.
Lift all to me.

Take time to review the vision
you have for your life.
Take time to pray.
Give yourself to me.

Feel the blessing of my love.
Open your heart to receive it.
Listen for guidance and direction.

Respond to others today from
your core of love.
They, after all, are you.

Take care of yourself today.

DAY 216

God, how can I be more loving today?

Watch where your ego wants to assert itself.
Notice what baggage you are carrying.

When you feel your less-than-best self taking
control,
    take a deep breath
     and ask yourself
      what the
        loving thing to do is.

When you notice the urge
    to be less than divine,
     breathe in love.

In that transformative moment,
    express your divinity
     by letting your words and actions
      come from a place of love.

Let go of pride
    and the need to be right.

Keep watch today
    and let your awareness
     find your hidden places.

Don't let your mind take over.
    Watch.
Give it all to me...and
    let love rule the day.

EVENING REFLECTION

Spirit really knows how to test us and challenge us to grow. If we are awake and aware enough, we can catch ourselves before we speak or act in less than loving ways. Spirit gives us a heads-up. We can recognize our arrogance, self-righteousness, or defensiveness as it shows up when we feel vulnerable, fearful, or inadequate.

When we feel our ego behaviour taking over, we have an opportunity to grab it, love it, and tell it that our higher spiritual being is now running things. We can breathe deeply and choose to act out of love.

I recognized that I was acting out of my ego many times today. Even in moments of casual conversation, I noticed that I sometimes wanted to put someone in their place, or demand respect, or show another who was boss, or be mean because it made me feel good. The baggage in my pockets wanted to spill out. This is the work that Spirit urges us to take on.

If we have the courage to face ourselves, to watch ourselves and be honest about ourselves, then we have a chance. Then we can change. Honesty leads to courage. Sometimes we even get angry at how we have behaved. Courage and anger can provide the incentives to become willing to change. And being willing ushers us into the grace and power of God.

DAY 217

God, how may I be of service today?

Seek to be more of what you really are...

You are of immortal divinity,
living the experience of
a mortal.

Remembering who you really are
and living into that reality
serves you and humanity
in countless ways.

More shining of your sacred light
and sharing of your love
would add to the evolving consciousness
of the whole world.

You want to serve?

Grow in your love.
Care for others.
Do not judge.
Seek peace.

Be compassionate,
patient,
kind,
and keep your heart open.

Serve me as I am...
the Transcendent Creator,
the Immanent Self,
the Christ Within...
and you serve the world.

DAY 218

God, what would you have me be like today?

Be like the cool early morning
on a summer day...
before the busyness begins.

Be calm, quiet, meditative.
Be patient, inviting, and open
to what may be.

See each event
as a sacred unfolding
of your path.

Look inside each encounter
to find its gift to you.

Receive the blessing
of each breath with gratitude,
and give of your best in
your decisions and actions.

Be like fresh air
and let your speech, gaze, and touch
be life-giving and rejuvenating.

May your light shine gently
on all you meet.

Yes...
Be like the early morning
on a summer day
and take those qualities
into the business and busyness
of your life
this day.

DAY 219

God, how would you have me grow today?

Keep learning today.
    Deepen your spiritual understanding.

Increase your appreciation of life
    by contemplating what a gift it is.

Let a new piece of knowledge
    sink into you.

Seek understanding...

Seek to expand your perspectives
    and the contexts of your insight.

Be humble,
    and honour what you don't yet know
or understand.

Allow love to
cascade down
    like a waterfall,
and rise up
    like a spring,
and meet
    and fill your heart.

May love splash
outward onto
your every word and action today,
    even as you learn to hold
and give more love;
    even as you expand the
boundaries of your heart
and deepen the
depths of your soul
so to hold more
of your own
divinity.

EVENING REFLECTION

After a full day of working and studying, I was preparing myself for a good night's rest when my wife told me excitedly of a wonderful expression for God she heard today. It was _Grow Or Die_.

I told her that it was interesting that she should hear that today. I relayed to her that my question to God that morning had been about growth. I then recited the first line of guidance that I had received: "Keep learning today."

It is exciting to recognize synchronicity when it occurs. Here was another sign along the way. It is as if God is winking or saying, "I see you...and you see me." Those small, seemingly insignificant coincidences are much more than they may appear to be. For those who pause to recognize the congruity of the moment with the larger context of the day, these markers become guideposts that encourage us to keep going the way we are going.

How did today's guidance influence your day?

DAY 220

God, how would you have me be in the world today?

Transcend intellect today
as best you can,
and allow me
to be master of your day.

Let your heart experience
    the divinity and majesty
        of my presence.

Let my presence fill you
as you open to my
love and grace.

    Breathe in my love.

As you exhale, let go of your belief
that your intellect is who you are.

Allow intuition and wisdom
to guide you
as your intellect becomes my divine servant,
    and your whole being
        an offering to my will.

DAY 221

God, how can I be more loving today?

Allow each person in your life
to be who they are
without judging them.

Today, just as you are your own
universe amongst universes,
    let each person's world
be what it is and unfold as it will,
without disturbing the process.

Notice when you are
jealous, angry, or self-righteous.

Let go of any need to control.
Instead, marvel at the complexities
of human existence
    and let me be God.

What does that mean?

It means that I have the world
and everything in it under my auspices.

So, let go and let God.

DAY 222

God, how can I be more loving today?

Do what brings healing.
Say what brings peace.

Remember your very nature
and connect all your actions
to this nature...of love.

Breathe in love,
    breathe out love.
Breathe in peace,
    breathe out peace.

Bathe your endeavours
in the light of highest purpose.
Dedicate your creative gifts to me
and offer them,
sacred and holy,
for the well-being of humanity
and the glory of all life.

This is not too much to ask.
You were created in love,
you exist in it, and you are called
to reflect this love
into the world.

Be love today
and the day will unfold with grace
and perfection.

EVENING REFLECTION

As soon as I completed the guidance this morning, I read the next chapter of a book that I am studying. It focused on aspects of spirituality found in parts of India. Then I proceeded to read the next installment in a book of stories and insights from around the world. Surprisingly, it turned out to be an inspirational story that took place in India! I thought it was quite a coincidence. But then I knew it was more than coincidence.

The story was about a man who prayed in the Ganges River daily. He was so kind that he took the trouble to lift a spider out of the water and set it on land. Before being set down, however, the spider bit the man. This went on for several days, the man rescuing the spider and the spider biting the man. Finally, the spider asked the man why he continued to rescue it when he knew he would get bitten, for, as the spider said, "This is what I do." The man replied, "And this is what I do."

The chapter I read, my own writing of the morning guidance, and this inspirational piece all converged on the theme of being who one is and doing what one does. As we grow in our spiritual lives, surprising coincidences and synchronicities become more frequent. They can happen so quickly and often that we begin to expect them without being surprised – although we continue to experience awe and wonder.

These markers are signs along the path; they let us know we are on the right track and in the flow and grace of our divine path. They encourage us to keep moving, growing, learning, and becoming.

Becoming what? Becoming more conscious of our divine being and letting it through with more awareness, letting it be who we are so that we can also say, "It is what I do."

DAY 223

God, what would you have me say and do today?

Today,
   do the work at hand.
Do not let others
deflect you from your path.

There is a time to attend to
your needs. A time to work and play,
a time to eat and pray, a time to
exercise and imagine.

Your path may be at odds with
another's, as each life
has a unique architecture.

This is why spiritual
gifts are necessary.

   Love, joy, peace, patience, kindness,
   goodness, gentleness, faithfulness,
   and self-control...

Keep these in mind as the day unfolds.

Today, do your own work.
Sense your soul's guidance and know that
I am drawing you toward your best.

Let go of all else and live in the
peace of my love and will.

DAY 224

God, what would you have me say and do today?

Do what your heart calls you to do today,
   and be at peace with your truth.

Carry your convictions humbly,
   and gracefully express understanding
when others would have you act differently.

   Then let go and give yourself to me.

Enjoy your ability to stand up for yourself.
Be even more joyful when you can place yourself
in another's shoes with genuine empathy.

Live in peace
with yourself and all whom you encounter today.

DAY 225

God, how can I be a more loving person today?

Concentrate on being in the moment.

Be fully present
to every person you encounter.
Pay attention.

Do not think of what
is next, or of what you just did.
Be present and alert
to what is proceeding now.

Trust your heart to respond
genuinely. Connect with it and
allow your benevolence to guide
your thoughts and actions.

Let your intuition guide
your timing and you will glide
through the day with grace and poise.

Be spontaneous
if your heart is saying yes.

Meetings and encounters are
never chance but are part of life's perfect
moment by moment unfolding.

Be present for everyone today.

DAY 226

God, how can I be more loving today?

Radiate love
born of the heart.
Connect to the place within
that holds deep regard for
every being.

Send forth this
esteem into the world.

Let your words honour the
inherent dignity in every person.
Let your actions
be gracious.

Let your voice carry
peaceful and calm tones;
let your movements
be fluid.

And may your love be
a balm for those who need
a healing touch today.

DAY 227

God, how may I be of service today?

Today,
   have faith
in my love and care.

   Walk the day's journey
in peace that comes from
knowing all is unfolding
as it should...
   that even the tragic
is accounted for.

      Let go of any
desire to control.
   Let go and allow me to perform
my works in you and through you.

      Serve the greater good
with power born of peace
that flows from faith.

Live in this faith and peace.

Do good in the world and let
that good find its place within the divine
tapestry.

Pray for all things today.
Send forth love.
Act with goodwill.

Be my ambassador today.

DAY 228

God, what would you have me be like today?

Be active for your cause today.

That is, do what you are called to do.
Do what nourishes you and brings you joy.

When something comes along that
might deter you,
let strength of purpose steady your aim.
   Let nothing throw you off today.

Follow your own lead.
March to the tempo of your own drum.
Dance to your own beat.
Move with your own rhythms.

Have confidence in your path,
      knowing that I honour you
    with providence,
  blessing, and
grace.

Enjoy walking your path,
  living your calling,
doing your sacred work,
   and being a holy advocate
for your cause.

DAY 229

God, how would you have me be in the world today?

Be watchful
   for anything that
tempts you away from living
the day in holiness.

Be aware
   of anything that
challenges or attempts
to thwart your behaviour
as a divine being.

Be vigilant
and remember who
   you really are.

Stay awake
to the habits
   that pull you into darkness.

Remember that what I
create is
   good, beautiful, and true.

Let me work in you today.
Remain in the light of
my power, wisdom,
and protection.

Let me move in you,
speak into you
and through you,
act within your being,
and guide your thoughts.

And watch
   with awe and wonder!

DAY 230

God, how can I be more loving today?

   All that happens
is brought forth by the energies
of the whole planet.
   Acts of love and kindness add
to the positive energy.
   Every act of kindness strengthens
the force of love.
   Your love effects blessings –
too many to count.
You are doing my great work.
   Today, stay aware of your
capacity to hold love.
   Let love inform your words,
your responses,
and your behaviour.
   Observe yourself diligently.
Try not to forget to remember
your awareness.
   If you catch yourself in moments of
shadow or forgetfulness,
gently reconnect to your heart
and think of me.
   Raise your spirit
and be the giver of love
that you truly are.

DAY 231

God, how may I be of service today?

Do your work
    in ways that bring
    you joy.
Work hard without
making it hard work.

The way is joy.

Working joyfully will imbue all that you do,
   all that you create,
     all that you accomplish,
       with joy's imprint, energy,
and blessings.

What blessings?

The blessing of easing another's pain,
   if only for a moment.
The blessing of revealing hopefulness,
   if only a glimpse.
The blessing of releasing a burden
   and offering a healing balm
     for the soul.

Yes!
Do your work in a
manner that imparts joy to
the world.

Let joy overflow the banks
of your being to spill its grace
over others today.

DAY 232

God, how would you have me be in the world today?

Be still...
like the waters of a lake on a
windless day.

Let nothing disturb
your peace.
Nothing.

Breathe easily and deeply
and let all things be.

Stay quiet and use your
deeper resonance when speaking.

    If disturbing winds begin
   to swirl around you,
move your consciousness
to a deeper place
where you can remain peaceful
and calm.

    The harder the winds blow,
   the deeper you go today.

The depths of your spirit
are limitless,
and you may always
find peace there,
no matter what
challenges the day brings.

Today, be an undisturbed lake...
    peaceful...
  deep...
still.

DAY 233

God, what would you have me say or do today?

Perform your duties
with excellence.
   Certainly, this should
always be the case, but today
you are to raise your
awareness in this endeavour.

Why?

So that inspiration can
pour itself into the energy
of your striving and increase
your creativity.

Excellence requires divine effort
and brings its own blessings.

Today, as you communicate with others,
perform your duties, handle your responsibilities,
and accomplish your tasks,
know you are part of
   the divine unfolding of
      perfect excellence.

   Nothing is insignificant.
   All thoughts, words, and actions are
part of today's exercise in excellence.

   Are you ready?

Excellent!

EVENING REFLECTION

I am writing this rather early today to capture a serendipitous event while it is fresh in my mind. After receiving and writing the day's guidance, I proceeded to pay some bills online and then began reading a book. I was waiting to receive a text from my wife informing me that she was finished with a meeting and would meet me for brunch.

Because of the guidance, I decided to go ahead to the restaurant and put my name in for a table, since there is usually a crowd there. I got a table and ordered us a beverage. When my wife called to see if I was ready to meet her, I told her I was already there and had gotten a table and ordered a beverage.

Do you know what she said? She said, "Excellent!"

DAY 234

God, how may I be of service today?

Be available.

Open yourself to others;
lend support
or encouragement.

Be ready, if called on,
to accompany or assist
someone in need.

Be attentive and
let your presence be felt.
See others through
your open heart
and welcome them with a warm smile.

Relax your body. Breathe deeply
and be ready for
the unfolding of the day.
Be available.
Be an angel on earth,
an ambassador of compassion,
a divine friend.

EVENING REFLECTION

For me, being available means setting aside my own agenda for a time. It means making space so that I can extend care and concern and give my time and energy for the sake of another. In our hectic society, narcissism and consumerism have great power and make it challenging to take the time to be there for others.

Availability asks the question, "Are we each other's keepers?"

Today, I witnessed a 14-year-old boy going into surgery. Waiting in the lobby was his best friend, who I learned had spent the night with his friend and then got up at 4:30 a.m. to accompany him on an hour-long drive to the hospital. He couldn't go into the operating room or the recovery room because he wasn't "family," but he proved himself to be family indeed, without the need for blood connection. He had heart connection. I witnessed the joy of these two young teens as they connected when the surgery was over.

Availability is of the heart. We adults have the reality of daily life with its inherent duties and responsibilities and so cannot always be physically available, even if we would like to be. But when we commit to being available, we find a way to connect, no matter what our life demands are. Connection may be via a phone call, text, or email to let another know we are thinking of them even if we are not in their presence.

It is one thing to say, "I'm available" and quite another to mean it and follow through. So in the final analysis, *integrity* is the secret ingredient in availability. It means that we mean what we say when we make ourselves...available. And when we are available, we are a true blessing indeed!

DAY 235

God, where would you have me grow today?

Be sensitive and gentle,
especially with yourself.

Accept with imperturbability
things you cannot control.

When others express themselves
in ways counter to your sensibilities,
practice letting it be,
without complaint.

Keep your peace.

Go about your day with the
clear intention of accepting
the world as it is
while you live in the
light and grace of who you are.

When surprises challenge your calmness,
breathe deeply and slowly
and give me your distress.

Let me hold you,
and all you carry.

Have faith.

DAY 236

God, how may I be of service, today? How can I
be more loving? What would you have me say
and do today? How would you have me be in the
world? Where and how would you have me grow
today?

So you want it all...?!

Then you must commit
to placing your whole being
– everything –
in me.

You must stay awake,
and aware of what you are
doing, feeling, saying, and thinking.

Then you will
hear my voice
and sense my guidance.
Your awareness is the
portal, the gate, through which
you receive wisdom.
All I am,
all my gifts,
are yours today.

If you lose yourself,
wake up again in me.
I am here, waiting
for your return.

Breathe deeply,
stay aware,
relax, and receive.

EVENING REFLECTION

When I sit down to ask God for guidance, I even ask to receive the question too. Sometimes the question is evident. Today it wasn't. Today I sat, and nothing came. I proceeded to write a question anyway, just to see how it felt. It became clear that I needed to write the next question, and then the next one, and so on. I chuckled to myself as I felt my soul saying, "Yes, you got it." The soul knows what it needs even when the mind doesn't. I suppose I needed all those questions addressed today. As the song goes, "Mama said there'd be days like this."

Talk about dancing with Spirit! The hardest part was following the lead of the guidance to stay aware and not get lost in forgetfulness. The art of acting demands similar self-awareness so that the actor can continuously pretend to be someone else. In committing to spiritual growth, the challenge is to pay attention to ourselves so that we can then pay attention to God's still, small voice, which pours forth wisdom and guidance.

Today was hit and miss. I had to reawaken my God-awareness many times. However, I felt grateful and blessed to be able to get back on board again and again. As intention forms our actions, I did experience longer and longer periods of self-awareness, particularly during conversations with others. I had a felt sense of how to respond, how to deliver my thoughts orally, and even how to move as I spoke.

Responding to our own awareness is not akin to being a puppet. It feels more like being an instrument of divinity. It is a beautiful feeling of having our Higher Power energize us, moment by moment.

How did you fare with this one today?

DAY 237

God, how may I be of service today?

Be a giver today.
  Do not desire anything for yourself,
for you have all you need in me.

Be the essence of my generosity,
  for I am always giving.

True giving understands the unity
  of all life.

You are giving to yourself
  when you give to others.

May your words give life,
may your actions give peace,
may your thoughts generate hope.
May you give light and love
without needing anything in return.

DAY 238

God, how would you have me be in the world today?

Imagine walking in nature
  on a sunlit morning.

Think of a mountain trail
  or a forest path.

Imagine walking slowly
  and taking in the scents of
    sweet grass, pine, wildflowers.

See small animals skirting your path
  and hear birds singing
    their morning songs.

Let the sylvan scene
  sink into you.

Carry this into your day.
Let it become your mien,
your way of being.

Today, walk your path
in the world
with a restful gait.

  Take the beauty of nature with you
into all the spaces you enter.

  Joyfully appreciate
having awakened
to this day.

  Sing your song today
to those you meet.

Be the nature of God today.

EVENING REFLECTION

I used a word in today's guidance that I just learned several days ago. It was the word *mien*, which means a person's look or manner. When I looked up the word on my computer's dictionary to make sure I had used it correctly, it turned out to be a wholly different word than I had thought. I was puzzled. I was sure that I had spelled the word correctly: *M-E-I-N*. I did not catch my own misspelling. I decided I would re-visit the issue when I sat down to write my evening reflection and went on with other work, which was mainly preparing for an event my wife and I were hosting that evening.

One of the things we had planned for this event was to play a board game I had created. As I was readying the word cards, I tried a new method of dealing the cards to the players – and out of more than 1,000 cards, the word I pulled was *mien*. I could hardly believe my eyes!

I was momentarily stunned at this...coincidence. Then I realized it could hardly be a coincidence. The odds of pulling that card were 1 in a 1,000! There was a higher power at work here that had worked on my behalf to make sure I got this word right – especially since the word was part of a spiritual text.

I shook my head, not in disbelief but in amazement. I was awed at the agency of God and God's ability to get through to me in this way. I was in a state of wonder at the power of divinity-at-work. I proceeded to correct the spelling in the guidance.

How did this happen? I sense it has to do with our intention, and the divine attraction it creates. Divinity knows where we are, what we are doing, and what we intend. Intention is a powerful force. It acts as a sort of spiritual magnet that draws to us the things we need to do our life work. It ushers in grace.

I thanked my angelic guardians for this divine bit of correction and carried on, once again affirmed in this effort. No matter how often I experience these serendipitous events, I never stop experiencing them as wonderful, awe-inspiring, stop-and-appreciate-what-just-happened occurrences.

Know what I *mien*?

DAY 239

God, what would you have me say and do today?

Do what pleases me.

Hold your tongue if
you would say something unkind.

Create peace with your words,
even if that is difficult.

Do the loving thing.
Be a blessing.

Pray for strength and
humility when you find that
you are frustrated.

Count your blessings today.
Remember my grace
in your life.

Know that present hardships
are temporary and meant to
test your spiritual resolve.

Breathe calmly through
the difficult moments of the day.

Keep your peace and know
that your angels
are sending love and encouragement.

You can live this day well.
Hold on to the best in you.
Hold on to me in you.

EVENING REFLECTION

It has been my experience that our spirit knows and appreciates our good acts. It resonates joy we can feel, joy that allows us to sense God's pleasure with us. I believe we are created as divine beings to be divine instruments of good. We can feel within us the profound difference between acting out of love and acting out of anything else. Television shows and movies are replete with dramas that encourage/normalize a violent response to life's vicissitudes. But the scriptures teach us that vengeance belongs to God. And God loves to forgive.

What pleases God is summed up in the golden rule: *Do unto others as you would have them do unto you.* Most of us learned the golden rule in grade school. It is still a powerful way to live. And if we did only that, I am sure God would be pleased.

DAY 240

God, how would you have me be in the world today?

Imagine first light
on a clear morning.
Imagine it breaking through
the mystery and peace
of the night.

See the first burst of sunlight
bringing brightness and hope,
and announcing a new day.

Be the beauty of dawn.
Be the hope of a new day.
When you face darkness and shadow,
remember the light you hold within and
let it shine forth.

Remember the dawn today
and let the light within you keep rising
as you greet those you encounter.
Let the glory and grace
of morning light
shine brightly into the world
as signs of God's love, light, and beauty.

Creative visualization is a powerful method of bringing the world into one's being. We are porous creatures. We can use our senses to bring the world into us and inform our actions and behaviour.

Dawn, with all its colour, beauty, and light, is a powerful image to bring into the body. The guidance encourages us to bring it into our being and live into it all day. This calls on our powers of imagination, visualization, and memory.

All life is energy, and we are too. This means we can connect with any energetic field and merge with it as much as our imagination and power of belief will allow us.

Today it was a privilege to carry within me the images from the guidance and sense the light within my soul rising to meet and greet each person and situation.

How did this guidance live in you today?

DAY 241

God, how would you have me be in the world today?

Be a soft wind
   that blows gently.

As you speak and move today
   do so with a lightness of being
   that comes from knowing
     I lift you up each morning
   and carry you through the day
   on the wind of divine grace.

Move with grace.
Demonstrate your trust in
my guidance.
Express faith in my
love and care for you.

     Relax your face muscles.
Relax your shoulders.

     Breathe in love...
Breathe out peace.

     Breath in soft...
Breathe out gentle.

     Breathe in peace...
Breathe out love.

     Breathe in gentle...
Breathe out soft.

     Be a soft wind
   that gently blows peace and love
through your encounters today.

DAY 242

God, how can I be a more loving person today?

Today,
take the focus off yourself.

Extend your energies outward.
     Speak to others from a place
of lightness of being that
comes from knowing
     I am taking care of you.

Let your heart be open to others.
Extend kindness in every encounter.

Appreciate the earth,
remembering that it
supports your very life.

See creation
as a gift of love.
See yourself
as a gift in the world.

Feel my love,
and bless everyone
you encounter today.

Are you ready?

DAY 243

God, what would you have me say and do today?

Rest in my peace.
      Practice handing over
your problems to my care.

      Let go today. Let go.

Say that you trust me.
      Say that you believe in my love for you.
If you even think these words,
      you open the door
and I can enter.

Look upon me with your
      heart open.

Move closer,
      and give me the burdens you carry.

Breathe them out,
      and let them go.
In return I will send
angels to encourage you.

I will bless you
      and uplift your spirit.
Receive me...
and let us venture this day together.

DAY 244

God, how would you have me be in the world today?

      Be quiet,
    like a body
of deep, still water.

      When you speak
    let your words surface
from the depths of your being –
the part closest to me.

Gather your words up from your centre
    and through your heart, where your
      inner truth dances with your mind
        and meets intention
      before being born
    into the world
as spoken word.

Speak today from a heart
    full of love and joy born of
      gratitude for all you
    have experienced as
blessing.

See past or present challenges
as blessings
that are meant to spur on
your spiritual maturity.

Let your inner quiet manifest
as the voice of beauty today,
      and may all you do be
      a reflection of
      the shining divinity
      and love you hold
      deep inside.

EVENING REFLECTION

Searching the depths of your soul for your words and then using your heart as a filter before speaking is an exercise in honesty and intention. Today, using the guidance, I found that I spoke much less, and when I did speak my words seemed to flow from a place of calm and divine connection. It was as if all the things I might have said were superfluous and guidance was inviting me to bypass them.

I found myself responding more honestly and supportively during casual conversations. When I sensed a judgment or a reflex opinion coming up, I was able to stop from blurting it out of my mouth. How? The image of a deep body of water allowed me to slow down and allow wisdom and kindness to moderate my words.

Our egos are complicated and often want to be boisterous and bold and take a no-holds-barred stance. We need to be aware of what our motivations really are, even when we are trying to be kind and humble. When we concentrate on our love and commit to accessing and manifesting it, we become more of the divine ambassador we are meant to be. And the power of love overcomes the power of our egoic behaviour.

How did you do with this today?

DAY 245

God, what would you have me say and do today?

Be the face of God to others
as you live this day.

Be unconditionally loving.

See the innocence in everything.

Let your voice
be calm and beautiful.
Let it flow from
your love for all creation.

Let your thoughts and actions
be generated by goodness.

And enjoy me
enjoying you
being the face of divinity
today.

DAY 246

God, how may I be of service in the world today?

Today,
  do not think much about
what to do or say, or how to serve.
Simply be and observe.

Still,
  let beauty be the compass
that guides you.

Be
  a beautiful flower unfolding
its petals without considering how.

Beauty
  is divinity manifesting.
It can be conspicuous, like a mountain's majesty
or a sunset's glory.

Be there for all to see –
  a joy to behold, refreshment for the soul,
a source of inspiration.

Today, simply be,
  and with your heart attuned to me
you will be beautiful.

Enjoy the magnificence of your beauty today.

DAY 247

God, what would you have me say and do today?

Today,
  be gentle
with yourself and
  all those you encounter.

Speak in calm tones
  using the deeper
resonance of your
  voice.

Use words that uplift and
  create joy and peace.
Let them
  be rich with gratitude and appreciation.

Today,
  do not complain.
Accept the day
  as it unfolds.

Where there is struggle,
  breathe peace and calm
into it and
  relax.

Remember that you are
  a divine being
created in love
  and held in grace.

Let the truth empower you.

Today,
  live gently, speak kindly,
and let your eyes sparkle
  with my delight in you.

EVENING REFLECTION

This was a doozy! Today was moving day, which comes with its own built-in stresses and challenges. I was moving a family member out of an apartment and putting things in storage while we searched for a new place for her to live during her last year of college. I would not say the morning started off gently, as we were not on the same page in terms of moving readiness.

I did have the thought that I should share the guidance, and I did. We both began laughing after the very first stanza as we realized we had already failed! Laughing brought a release for us both, and we then apologized to each other and began again.

It seems amazing to me how using the deeper register in my voice can help keep me calm and centred. We both enjoyed the yoga of consciously using the deeper range of our voices, and we laughed a lot as we recognized the effects and blessing of doing so.

It is easy to find things to complain about on a moving day. For example, there were moments of frustration while trying to get a large couch down a set of narrow stairs with a 90-degree turn. When one of us complained, we reminded the other of the guidance's encouragement to NOT complain. We would say, in our deepest, lowest voices, "Are you complaining?" Then we would laugh our complaints away. And there were also many moments of breathing in peace and calm.

Now, that third stanza – to uplift and bring peace with our words – was rich in challenge. A roommate was moving out at the same time and had a couple of people helping out. They were struggling to move two heavy couches down the narrow stairs and had no dolly to wheel the couch away once they had accomplished that daunting task. They argued about how best to move the couches and who should or shouldn't be telling the others what to do. It was uncomfortable. Then I found out they were all family. I felt a nudge to offer my help to ease the physical strain I saw in the three women, and they gladly accepted. Not only did my added strength help, but my joy in assisting them seemed to affect all involved. Suddenly the work of moving transformed from burden to celebration, all while we huffed and puffed.

We ended up with our eyes sparkling and our beings alight with the grace we experienced in one another. It took a while to get there, but we got there.

How did you move through the day?

DAY 248

God, how can I be more loving today?

Let patience be your mantra.

Be accommodating and supportive.

Breathe slowly and deeply
    when you feel impatient.
Live at the speed of faith today
    and trust my wisdom.

When you do something for another,
    give it your complete attention
    and do it as an offering
    of goodness and goodwill.
Expect nothing in return
    and receive the joy of
    selfless service.

Be a good listener.
Refrain from speaking until
    a response is called for or asked for.
Speak from a place of respect,
    and honour the truth of the other's
    perspective and experience.

Keep your heart open,
    your eyes bright with delight,
    and your mind attentive,
and watch with joy how you become
a blessed saint
this day!

DAY 249

God, how may I be of service today?

Begin by serving yourself today.

Give to yourself by taking the time to read
and contemplate this guidance.

As you shower or bathe
really feel the warm water on your skin.
Appreciate the gift of cleanliness.

Do not rush through your breakfast.
Offer gratitude for its nourishment with each bite.

Acknowledge the innate value
of everyone you encounter today.

See beauty in every face and
in every action or behaviour.

When you feel disappointment, be generous of
heart. Make room for others' shortcomings,
remembering your own humanness.

Work with joy today, keeping in mind
the good you are adding to the world.

At day's end, give thanks for your gifts and skills,
and for the opportunities you have had to add
to the beauty of life today.

And take time to reflect on and appreciate those
who have blessed you with beauty and joy today.

DAY 250

God, how would you have me be in the world today?

Imagine yourself as the canopy
        of blue sky
dotted with fluffy clouds
        blown across the heavens
by the gentle celestial breeze
        that brings peace and repose.

As you journey through this day
imagine those you meet
to be within this powerful picture.

When you are present with
this image, your energy
becomes an oasis
of refreshment and rejuvenation.

It will be your unspoken gift
to all you meet;
a gift of love for them
from the depths of
your own love.

        And thus, you will
bless your own soul.

DAY 251

God, how can I be more loving today? Where would you have me grow?

Take it easy on yourself today.
Remember that you are a fallible human.

When you don't measure up to your own expectations, keep that in mind – and forgive yourself.

How?

Live today knowing that you are still growing and transforming – becoming more beautiful with every stumble, with every lesson learned...
again, and again...

DAY 252

God, what would you have me say and do today?

Today...
stay in your heart flow.

Sense when you need some quiet
and find a way to provide it for yourself,
even if only for a few minutes.

Receive with warmth of spirit
those who seek you out.

Pay close attention:
Is inspiration trying to reach you?

Be grateful for your life
and appreciate those you love
and those who love you.

Make someone laugh today.

Applaud at least one person just for being
the beautiful soul they are.

Let your eyes smile into theirs.

Rest your being in my divine care today
and watch the day's petals
unfold into a beautiful flower.

DAY 253

God, what would you have me say and do today?

As you live this day,
   take in the beauty around you
and reflect it back in
   all you do.

Today...
see the sun and
   reflect its warmth and light.
Notice the clouds and
   reflect their softness.
Breathe the air and
   reflect its life-giving qualities.
Be the beautiful soul
that you are.

Let your words be
rich with grace.
Let the divinity within you
take centre stage and guide you.

Take a moment to feel
your own holiness,
and then let it touch someone.

Stay thoughtfully present
to me
and be open and willing to
follow guidance.

Will you do this today?

DAY 254

God, how would you have me be in the world today?

Be your Self –
   the divine within your physical body.

Sense this true you
   beneath your surface feelings and emotions,
   under the deep issues of your psyche,
   below the wounds, fears, and mistakes that
     come with life's ups and downs.

Go beyond and touch
   the purity and the pureness of you,
   the *you* created in my image.

Become conscious of this light-being
   who is untouched by the harshness of life,
   who is full of love and beauty,
   who ceaselessly makes available the resources
     that allow enjoyment
     while withstanding life's challenges.

You are a holy being.
Live today as a holy one, born of God,
blessed and pure, wise and humble,
full of peace, love, and joy.

DAY 255

God, how may I be of service today?

Do what is in front of you.

Move forward through the day with vigour,
knowing you are fulfilling your life purpose.

Be thankful for all you are,
and for the privilege of sharing your gifts
with others.

Offer all you are to the day.
Give joyfully and let go of the results.

Let all your words come from a place
of unconditional love,
and let all your actions
express goodness.

Do something to nourish your own
health and happiness.

Today,
know that you are adding beauty
and grace to all life.

EVENING REFLECTION

For those on the spiritual path, it can be tempting to think that we have to do – or at least attempt to do – something...big. But that is far from the truth. An act that we consider to be small can have a tremendous effect. We may not always get to see the results. But sometimes we do.

Today I thought I would work on several projects in a major exercise of multi-tasking. But that first line of the guidance kept ringing in my soul: *Do what is in front of you.* And I *had* been putting off what was in front of me. It was a promotional video that I do monthly to promote an event my wife and I host. Although I still had plenty of time to get it done, I *felt* a nudge to go ahead and do it *now*.

I had no sense of why Spirit would be nudging me so, but I went ahead and did it. I decided to do it as a sacred offering and poured myself into the process for the hours it took. When I finally took a break on the front porch, I enjoyed the beauty of the day and the company of my children.

For the benefit of my health and happiness I thought I might exercise – but it didn't happen. I felt I should keep working to finish this project. Instead, I ate a bowl of delicious chicken curry. Since it is easy for me not to eat when I am working, this was absolutely doing something good for my health and happiness.

So here's the upshot: I finished the video and emailed it to my wife, who was out of the country. It was midnight my time and 8:00 a.m. where she was. She called, surprised I had finished the project so early. It so happened that the video was just the medicine she needed at that moment. Her gratitude was evident, and we shared a beautiful time together. That made the whole effort worth it. And I got to see the reason for the nudge to complete the work. That is grace in action.

What is in front of you that you need to get done? What are you being nudged to do?

DAY 256

God, how can I be more loving today?

See my face in all you encounter today.
Feel my love for everyone you meet.
Hear my words in everything you say.

See creation as a
gift of my love, and
    let it be your love.

Treat everyone as a precious jewel
within the setting of life.

Love grows with each outpouring of
divine intention to love.
    There is no limit.

Live me into all you say and do today.
And let love flow from us into
every living being and
every circumstance and challenge.
Let love become the power that
informs all we do,
because it is who we are,
together, as one.

DAY 257

God, how would you have me be in the world today?

Imagine a cool breeze
on a summer day.
The heat of the sun warms,
    and the breeze refreshes.

As you live this day, let the
    warmth and refreshment
within you come through.

Let the warmth
    of your heart be felt.
Let your
peace and grace be seen.

Let your inner joy flow
    like a fresh mountain breeze.
    May it be heard in the tones
and melodies of your voice.

Warmth and refreshment...
    today's gifts from you
to all who come
    into your life.

DAY 258

God, where would you have me grow today?

I would have you deepen
the intimacy we share.

Today, keep your mind on
our relationship and our mutual
love for each other.

Ask me for wisdom
and I will give it.
Pray with me
and I will guide you.

Make the time to
be with me in solitude.
Then take me with you
to all your activities.

Let me work with you,
and when you eat or rest,
let me sit with you.

Today, let us be intimate,
that the world may become even more divine
through our bond.

DAY 259

God, how may I be of service today?

Do today
what, in the depths of you,
you hear and feel and sense.

Perform your duties and responsibilities
with excellence and reverence.

Let me be part of everything
you seek to accomplish today.

Open yourself
to my grace.

Today, as a co-worker in
the Divine Work,
listen for my guidance.

DAY 260

God, what would you have me say and do today?

Watch closely today
    for there are things meant just
    for your eyes,
    that only you can attend to.

      Perhaps you will catch the eye
of a hurting soul and smile.
      Maybe you will save the life of
    a small trapped insect.

Remember that no act is insignificant
    when done with love and care.
      Each act of kindness is its
    own miracle...
and each deepens your spirit.

Today there are some miracles that
    only you can perform.
      When you recognize the moment,
    open your heart
and be a hero of love.

EVENING REFLECTION

Not long after writing this guidance, as I was sitting at my desk, I noticed an insect crawling on the screen of the door to the patio. I watched it for a moment, trying to figure out what it was. It was walking back and forth, and I wondered what it was trying to do. I had seen bees and wasps check out the area for nesting sites, but this insect was different.

I got up from the desk to have a closer look. That is when I was able to see that the insect was on *my* side of the screen. It was looking for a way *out*. I opened the screen and guided the creature out. As it flew away, I felt good that I had just helped one of God's beings. Now it could get on with its life and purpose.

We all can find our way into situations that hinder our forward motion. Sometimes we are lucky enough to have others take notice of us and give us a hand to get back on the right track. And as we help others, whether insect, animal, or human, we become heroes of life itself.

DAY 261

God, what would you have me say and do today?

Move forward,
   but stay centred in me.

Whatever adventures you embrace this day
do not forget me in them.
Hold to your divine centre.

Remember that nothing happens outside
of my purview.
There is no place I am not; and in that
knowing is hope, blessing, and comfort.

Today, remember that I am
   wherever you are.

Move forward in confidence with
my centering love.

DAY 262

God, how would you have me be in the world today?

Today, practice
putting your complete trust in me...
remembering that I am peace, stillness, and joy.

This means fear and worry
are banished.
The body has its own reactions
and instincts,
   but you are more than your body.
You are spirit.

Let the strength and faith of your spirit
flow through your heart.

Today, practice staying awake
and conscious of your mind/body reactions
and then let yourself choose your response.

Surrender your will to mine.
Then, inside the sanctity of your soul,
go to where I am
      and commune with me.

Sense my will.
Trust me to speak through
your mind, intellect, soul, and spirit.

And, trusting this connection,
   live this day in confidence,
knowing that you are guided
by the one who loves you unconditionally
and works for your highest good.

DAY 263

God, how may I be of service today?

Be ready to support anyone
who needs your assistance today.

That means opening your
heart and allowing your
own agenda and plans to
wait if necessary.

Selflessly serving another
is a spiritual act.

When you genuinely give yourself
to another's cause without judgment,
you practice unconditional love.

Today, breathe in love,
breathe out service...and be ready.

Sometimes, serving
means staying out of the way,
giving space, or being quiet.

At other times it means
paying close attention and
offering whatever is needed.

As you extend your giving heart
today, feel my love emanating.

Enjoy me smiling in you
as you assist and support others.

Are you willing to do that
today?

EVENING REFLECTION

9:00 a.m.
Not ten minutes after I wrote today's guidance, I was challenged to fulfill it!

As I was preparing to go for a morning workout, it dawned on me that someone close to me might benefit from a guidance that had come earlier. It was still in my handwriting, which can be hard to read sometimes. I had to decide whether or not to stop, put my agenda aside, type the guidance, and get it to the person. I knew they were about to embark on a long day of training that would require much fortitude.

Well, I did type the guidance. I attached a note that said to read the guidance before getting out of the car to go to the training, and that it should be kept in a pocket, as its energy could still have an effect. However, when I delivered it, the person threw me a curve. She said she didn't know if she would have time to stop and read it and wondered if I could just read it aloud.

I could and did.

She thanked me and said she felt somewhat better and more encouraged, and that she would try to "hold on" to the message of the guidance during the training.

If we feel a certain pull to help someone and our help is accepted, that is all we can do. The rest is not up to us. Sometimes we get to know if our help really helped, and sometimes we don't. In this case, it was communicated to me that this guidance made a positive difference in the person's day.

As a writer of daily inspirations, I am always grateful when what comes through has been of benefit to another. It is one way I support and assist others in the adventure of life.

DAY 264

God, what would you have me say and do today?

Practice the art of taking your time.
Do not rush anything
or rush through anything.

Let each event have its own life.
Pay attention to even small details,
and allow all your activities to speak to you
and give you their gifts.

Watch how you live today, and
move at a pace conducive to your
peace and calm.

Speak only when necessary and
say only what is needed. Rest your
mind as much as you can.

Do not think much on any one thing
unless it be the gift of your life or
the beauty and majesty of creation.

Follow the air in
through your nose and down into your lungs as
you inhale.
Marvel at this life-giving act
and give thanks.
Fill the atmosphere
around you with gratitude as you exhale.

Take your time today.
Relax,
and embrace your life
moment by moment.

DAY 265

God, what would you have me say, do, or be like in the world today?

Let your spirit rise to meet every situation
with grace.

Live this day with
humility and in peace.
Bring a spirit of love and fellowship
to all.

Remember that you are the face
and body of divinity.
Your words reveal me.
I move through you,
and in you – as you.

Be my grand ambassador of
love and peace today.

DAY 266

God, what would you have me say, do, or be like today? How would you have me grow today?

Today,
    be strong in your faith.
Let go of worry.

Let go of things you cannot
    control, and seek guidance
for the things you can influence.

Remember the obstacles you have
    overcome in the past,
and the challenging situations that
have worked themselves out over time.

Today,
    invoke patience and resolve.
Take one step at a time.
Give each action to my care.

Breathe slowly and deeply...
relax into divine will.

Know that all will be well...and is.

Let your intentions
    be immersed in love.

Have faith
    and let my peace embrace you.

Will you do these things today?

EVENING REFLECTION

For me, being strong in faith means believing what I cannot yet see. Letting go of worry means giving over outcomes to a higher power and being okay with that. As the saying goes, all you can do is all you can do. My father used to say, "Keep on living and see what happens." Life is an adventure. And it can be like going down class 5 rapids in a rubber raft with a group of people, a paddle, and a guide. Even though it may be dangerous, we do it for the fun of it and for the thrill of it. We ride the source of raw power to where it takes us.

In some ways, God is the same: an incredible source of raw power taking us down the river of life. Ride the currents of life knowing that God is the river, the boat, the guide, and the incredible scenery along the way!

DAY 267

God, what would you have me say, do, or be like today?

Be joyful!

Joy arises as we feel
    gratitude and appreciation
        for the gift of life.

Today,
  let joy
      shine in your eyes.
  Let it be heard in
your soft chuckles.

Joy need not be demonstrative
or overpowering.

    Let it simmer in your soul,
  let it gentle your listening,
let it dance in your walk,
and sing in your words.

    Let joy clothe you in its radiance,
  fill you with its power,
and shine its brightness
through your being today.

DAY 268

God, what would you have me say, do, or be like today?

Today,
keep things simple.

    Smile.
    Laugh.
    Look people in the eye.
    Mean what you say.
    Tip the server.

Notice the beauty of the day,
no matter the weather.

    Pray for someone.
    Give someone a hug.

Notice your breathing,
then take a few deep
breaths in gratitude
for your life.

    Be kind.
    Use your soft voice.
    Forgive.
    Let childlike awe and wonder reach you.
    Love.
    Give thanks to God.

Simple, right?

DAY 269

God, where would you have me grow today?

Stay in your heart.
　　You and I unite there.

In all your endeavours today
let your consciousness
　　find the ground of
　　your heart.

Listen for my guidance.

Feel the nudge of
inspiration as it
　　lights the fire
　　of your creativity.

Let your intuition receive
my subtle communications.

Let this day be a
　　joint venture
– a co-creation of you and me.

And as we live and move
within each other, there will
come a moment when we won't be able to
tell us apart.

Are you ready?

DAY 270

God, how may I be of service today?

Today...
give your time to those
who need a listening ear.

Patiently, and with genuine interest,
　　take in the heart of another.
Listen with full attention
　　and respond with love and encouragement.
Ask wisdom to guide your words.

Let your willingness to be there
　　for another be enough.
Ask for nothing in return.

Look for opportunities to support
　　those who need help.
Be available.

Selfless service
　　blesses the world.
Let your inner light shine forth
　　like a divine beacon that lets others know
you are there to help.

Are you willing to do this today?

DAY 271

God, how can I be a more loving person today?

Keep your heart open
   and ready to love.

    Lift someone up with encouraging
words and your gentle presence.

Breathe deeply and quietly
   to ground and centre yourself.
     Today, stand with another.
   Be that person's champion.
Be a light in their darkness.
Be the blessing they need.

DAY 272

God, what would you have me say and do today?

Lift another's spirit
   out of loneliness, despair, or frustration.

   Ask me for the words and
   trust your good heart.

I am with you all the time.
   Let this give you strength.

Remember your own moments
   of major growth
   and share them with someone
   who may need an inspiring story.

Offer hope based on your
   experiences. Be encouraging,
   and let your joy come through.

Give hope today
   to someone in need.

DAY 273

God, how would you have me be in the world today?

Be a rock for someone to lean on today.
　　And yet...be a soft place to land as well.

How?

Be ready to listen patiently.
　　Speak gently and lovingly.
　　　　Repeat what you hear
　　　　so that it is clear you understand
　　　　　　what is being communicated.

　　　　　　Then let your faith
　　　　move you as you offer words of
　　hope and encouragement.

Offer your successes in life as examples
　　of a new vision,
　　　　a new way of life.

Yes...today be strong, soft, solid, and gentle.

DAY 274

God, how would you have me be in the world today?

Be warm.
　　Let your words be filled with
　　　　light and love.

Don't rush to speak;
　　let your thoughts become
　　　　words that are genuine.

Use eye contact and
　　gentle touch to add power
　　　　to your caregiving.

Let your moods and actions
　　be infiltrated by
　　　　my divine light.

Serve the greater good.

Ask yourself what the most loving
　　thing to do is in each circumstance
　　　　you find yourself in.
Then...do it.

Remember that I am the
light of your being.
　　Stay conscious of this
　　　　connection and let my
　　warmth, love, and beauty
fill you, moment by moment.

EVENING REFLECTION

Today I attended a gathering where previously I had felt uncomfortable and like an outsider. The guidance to be warm and make eye contact was amazingly helpful as I spoke with people. I didn't rush to speak (which I have done in the past as a way to feel less like an outsider) but waited until I sensed a natural opening in the conversation.

The admonition to let myself be filled with God's warmth, love, and beauty was amazingly effective. I concentrated on directing my attention to those qualities flowing into me. I could feel myself allowing them to come into me, pass through, and flow outward.

I ended up having a very enjoyable time, thanks to the grace of Spirit and my willingness to use the spiritual resources always available to me.

How did this guidance unfold in your day?

DAY 275

God, what would you have me say, do, or be like today?

Be easygoing today.
   Take everything in stride.
      Let nothing ruffle your feathers.
         Accept the events of the day.

Let your words be positive
   and supportive.
      Let your actions express a
joyful mood.
      Laugh.
   Play.
      Breathe.
   Keep your shoulders relaxed.
      Smile.

See beauty in everything today.
      Have fun.
     Be...easygoing.

Yes, be easygoing today.

DAY 276

God, what would you have me say and do today?

Keep yourself in a state of quiet love this day.

Tend your own spirit.
Read something inspiring or enlightening.
Review a personal journal,
or begin one.

Feel into what may be calling you today.
It may be something entirely new.

Take a few minutes to pray for yourself
and your loved ones.

If any negativity comes up, acknowledge its
presence without judgment,
then filter it back
    to your heart of love
and let it rest there
    in that healing energy.

Today, keep the peace.
Support the manifestation and maintenance
of harmony and peace.

Let the quiet beauty of your love
emanate gentleness,
and may the lightness of your being
bring joy, healing, and peace to all those who
need it.

EVENING REFLECTION

An interesting thing happens when I quiet down –
when I allow myself to speak less and take in more.
Other senses come to the fore and exhibit their gifts
more obviously. Hearing and observation skills become more acute and I can check in with myself in a
more in-depth manner.

I attended a gathering where I was the new face
among a group of people who had known each other
for some time. The shell around this community group
was not easy to crack. I took a moment to pray for
myself and for those whom I was meeting. I worked
on my own inner world and chose to exude warmth
and love instead of fear. It allowed me to filter,
through a loving heart, the negativity I was antici-
pating. I decided to enjoy myself and be myself no
matter what. I spoke without expecting much in return and had faith that I was in the right place at
the right time. I ended up enjoying the event much
more than I would have had I bought into negativity and fear.

Emanating gentleness, beauty, and love changes our
energy and our response to others. Even if it does not
change others, it changes us – which makes all the
difference.

DAY 277

God, what would you have me say and do today?

Be sensitive to the feelings of others
and respond accordingly.
    Your strength of spirit will allow you to do this.

Practice hospitality for its own sake.
    Do not take offence.
    Forgive any perceived wrongs.

Give me your day.
    Pray for upcoming encounters,
      foreseen and unforeseen,
    that your heart may be prepared
to be open and generous.

Let your spoken words
    be comforting and supportive.
      Put yourself in the other person's shoes
and let compassion guide your speech.

Today, you will be a source of healing,
understanding, and peace.

    Are you willing?

DAY 278

God, what would you have me say and do today?

Rise up in spirit
    that you may serve
      the greater good.

Anchor your heart in
    good works, out of love for others.

See every person you encounter
    today as part of you,
      and care for that person
as you would care for yourself.

Let your words honour
    and encourage;
      be patient in your manner
    and gentle in your tone of voice.

As you do these things today,
    as you rise to serve the
      greater good,
    know that the greater good
will also rise to serve you.

DAY 279

God, what would you have of me today?

I would have your love.

Today, I would have you wrap
the earth and all beings
in your love.

Let your love flow to every person,
to all animals and insects,
amphibians and fish.

Let the grass, flowers, trees,
and earth receive your loving
energy.

See all as part of you,
and treat all with dignity, respect, and
love.

For love is your essential nature,
and this is what I would have of you
today.

Let your love flow
with joy, courage, humility, and
gratitude.

Today we will pour out our love onto the
world together...and miracles will
happen.

EVENING REFLECTION

Sometimes spiritual growth is a haphazard process,
or so it seems.

Today I walked into an office supply store I frequent.
There was a new person working there. I had hardly
stepped through the door before I was asked if I was
looking for something in particular. I was immediately irked. I avoid stores where the salespeople assault you upon entry as if you can't find what you're
looking for without assistance. My response was, "No,
I got it," which made no sense since I was looking
for something specific. My tone was not loving and
elicited a response that was equally unloving.

I had failed at being loving...again. But I did galvanize my internal forces to stay awake to the possibility that more tests were awaiting me. That didn't
happen until I was writing this reflection and a stink
bug showed up on my desk. A stink bug! I had to
laugh a little as I imagined karma getting back at
me for my earlier, stinky attitude. You reap what you
sow, right? And the harvest can come in many forms.
So for me? A stink bug from God. What a sense of
humour.

And a chance to love.

I slipped a piece of paper under the bug and then
gently set it outside. Love conquered in the end.

DAY 280

God, how may I be of service today?

Take care of your mind.

Just as the body needs
food, rest, exercise, and play,
the mind also needs to be cared for.

How?

Feed it healthy thoughts.
Read inspiring words.
Listen to music that
touches your soul.

Do not listen to foolishness.
Turn off the radio or television
when the banter or images
do not nourish
your heart centre.

Deepen your understanding
of who you are;
do not let the world label you,
for you are beyond description.

Breathe and allow your mind
to take an extended break from
burdens, responsibilities, and duties.
They will be there...

Today, take care of your mind –
your beautiful, divine, holy,
God-gifted mind.

And by so doing
you will serve humanity by
being a ready instrument
for divine purposes.

DAY 281

God, how may I be of service today?

Be a good steward of your gifts and talents –
from your smile to your manner of being,
from your innate talents and skills
to those you have developed with hard work over
time.

Be wise with your time today.

Work with conscious purpose,
keeping in mind those who will
benefit from your endeavours.

Leave any doubts about your efforts
with me.

Be confident with the gifts
you have received.
Stay connected to the source of
who you are
and be at peace with who you are.

Today...
offer your gifts in service to the world.

DAY 282

God, how would you have me be in the world today?

Be powerful.
  BE POWERFUL.
    B E   P O W E R F U L...!

Spiritual power
  exists and acts out of love
    for all creation.

When you tap into your spiritual power
    you have a heart of love,
  and no fear in the face of evil.
    You have a mind that is
  peaceful, clear, and filled with
divine light, grace, and protection.

Spiritual power is life-giving power beyond
  despair and destruction.
It gives hope; it heals,
  and makes whole.

Today, be true power, not worldly force.
Be the power of light and love.

Will you do this?

DAY 283

God, how would you have me be in the world today?

Be a bridge of hope and light
  for those looking for ways
    to move from pain to joy,
    from dark nights to bright days.

Perhaps you will not know who these people are
    but they will see your light and
      move toward the beacon you shine.

You may not hear back about your good work,
  or how you kept another hopeful.
You may not be told how your smile
  and words of encouragement
    kept someone from sinking further
      into discouragement or despair.

    But that's okay.
    Being a divine instrument
  brings its own rewards.

Today
let the warmth of love, the light of hope,
  and the power of faith be strong in you.
Let the remembrances of past blessings
  fill you with gratitude and appreciation.

And you can be a bridge to
  transformation for someone
    wanting to move into light, love, healing,
    peace,
      and freedom.

DAY 284

God, what would you have me say and do today?

Be present.

Practice being fully in the moment
without thinking about the past or the future.

Live deeply in each moment.

Focus on the person with whom
you are talking.
Be fully attentive.
Really listen. Do not anticipate.
Respond from a place of compassion, camaraderie,
and love.
Nourish your own loving heart today:
with gratitude, by remembering how blessed
you are,
with appreciation, by remembering kindnesses
shown you,
with humility, by remembering times of grace,
with joy, by remembering how it feels to
be loved.

Today, be present and connected with love.
Appreciate every being as precious,
and patiently give them your time.

EVENING REFLECTION

I spoke with a friend today by telephone. He was going
through some hardships that made certain duties difficult to fulfill. He said to me that all he hoped for was to
be able to "be present" for others.

It occurred to me to offer the meditation guidance, which
I did. As I read the last two stanzas to my friend, I could
hear an audible, "Hmm..."

Hearing about nourishing love through gratitude, appreciation, humility, and joy connected with my friend
in a way that allowed him to move closer to the present
now and away from the cloudy fog he had been in.

My friend thanked me for offering the reading, and I
wished him well. I suppose you could say I had followed
the guidance myself, which allowed me to be present in
such a manner that I could be of help. And for that I am
grateful.

How did the day's guidance go for you?

DAY 285

God, how would you have me be in the world today?

Open your eyes.
See me in all things today.

When you look at others,
see me in them. I am the same
me in them as in you.

Relate to me in them,
for we are all each other.
Be friendly and kind to others,
for you are treating us
as you treat them.

I am always here,
watching and loving in you, as you.

As we look through
each other's eyes,
we will see a day of miracles.

EVENING REFLECTION

Today I spoke with someone who felt distanced from
the world. She told me that everything felt better
when her eyes were closed. I felt an inner urge to
offer this guidance, which I had just written. It is
amazing to see what unfolds when we follow Spirit's
lead. Here was a person who wanted to close her eyes
to feel better, and the guidance was about opening
our eyes to see God in all things. The person acknowledged the divine timing of the message and
the hope it offered.

The conversation affirmed once again for me that when
writing inspirational books and resources I can only
do what I am called to do. What happens with the
work is not up to me. And it is always humbling to
hear or know that what has come from inspiration
has been useful to someone else.

How did the day's guidance unfold for you? What miracle occurred?

DAY 286

God, how can I be more loving today?

Place your desires into my hands.

Work your work with diligence
    and purpose,
and perform your tasks
    with excellence.

When advice and suggestions
    come your way,
whether asked for or unsolicited,
    listen with open mind
and loving heart
    for whatever gift you may be receiving.

Always seek wisdom during your
    decision making.

Believe in yourself and
    trust the intelligence
within you.

Be at peace today with
    who you are,
how far you have come,
    what you have accomplished,
and what you are striving for.

Above all... remember that my love
    surrounds you.

EVENING REFLECTION

As a creative artist, I receive feedback on projects I have in development. Sometimes I invite the feedback, and sometimes I get a surprise offering – usually at the end of the day when I am tired and have run into someone who sees an opportunity to offer insight.

This may be the reason this guidance came up this morning. I had been at an event and was preparing to leave when someone offered some perspectives on a new project I was working on. They had seen my working model and wanted to give me some suggestions. I listened, but cannot say I was very receptive, though I remained polite. However, I slept on it and did find value in what had been offered. I called the person and left a message thanking them for being willing to offer their thoughts on fine-tuning the project. I apologized for perhaps not seeming very receptive at the time and closed by again offering my gratitude.

Actually, that short, unexpected encounter proved valuable, as I dreamt that night of major improvements I could make to the project – improvements I hadn't seen even after months of work and development. Perhaps I was only now ready to receive the cherry on top.

You never know where angels are going to come from, or when, or how.

How did this guidance unfold in your day?

DAY 287

God, how would you have me be in the world today?

Today, practice allowing only positive
thoughts to grow in your mind.

Do not let negativity find fertile ground in you.
Notice it but don't give it room to grow.
    Instead, expose yourself to positive influences.
Invite them to stay. Nourish them.
    Think of my love.
        Seek peacefulness.
            Find calmness.

Do not watch or listen to
violent media images.
    Not today.

Give your soul a blessed day
of all things loving and life-giving.
Listen to music that uplifts,
words that inspire.
    Be diligent in this today.

Greet negativity with kindness and let it go.
Make yourself a place
    of peace on earth.

DAY 288

God, what would you have me say and do today?

Stay aware.
    Try to be awake
        to what is going on
    in and around you today.

Yes, this takes effort
    and willingness.
And it allows you to
    know what to do.
It lets
    divine wisdom and guidance get clear.
Mistakes are fewer
    and difficulties more often avoided.

The light of divinity can
    shine on all your
        endeavours because you
    have not fastened on the blinkers
of past and future.

Yes, today, to the best of your ability,
    stay awake to yourself,
        aware of all things.
        Let love and light
    inform all you say
and do.

DAY 289

God, what would you have me say and do today?

As you journey through this day,
   concentrate on each activity
as you engage in it.
   Be as present as you can be
so that you take it in fully
   and are open to all it
has to offer.

See beneath the surface
   and enjoy its gift to you.

When you speak today,
feel how your words flow
   from soul to heart to mind
and out into the world.

Take care to be aware
   of what you are communicating.
Make effort to ensure that all you say
   comes without ill intent.

Today let your words be rich in love.
Concentrate on letting
   your divinity shine through,
so that all you say and do
   is filled with light,
compassion, and grace.

EVENING REFLECTION

Concentration is a tool that we learn to use over time. The practice requires a willingness to keep focusing our attention toward a certain intention. It was a beautiful experience for me today to pay attention to heart, mind, and soul and then watch which words and actions bubbled up as a result of my intention to love, my will to be present to love's guidance, and my desire to express the guidance.

Many of us are not aware of what we do or say until after the fact, when it can be too late and what we have said or done in haste has caused damage. Much of what we say and do arises from reaction and rote response inculcated by culture, peer pressure, media, or society at large. But the gift of concentration begins to free us from unconscious behaviour so that we see beneath the surface of situations – and ourselves – and choose actions that do not hurt or harm.

How did you do with today's guidance?

DAY 290

God, what would you have me say and do today?

Use your power
with love and humility.
All beings have power.
Power comes with being.
As _____ (name your job or role)
you hold and steward power.

Make your decisions from a stance of love.
Consider the common good in each situation.

Be aware of your anger or passive-aggressive
feelings,
and pause and contemplate the source.
Bring your feelings into the light and
wash them
with understanding, insight, love, and
forgiveness.

Let your intention be
to empower others.

Encourage...support...affirm.

Give those you engage with the opportunity
to demonstrate their skills and talents.

Let your power be divinely powered
with the grace of love and light –
and watch what happens.

DAY 291

God, how would you have me be in the world today?

Imagine that you are one
with everything today.

Everyone you see and
talk to is you,
so that whatever you say,
you say to yourself...
whatever you do,
you do for or to yourself...
whatever you think,
you put those thoughts upon yourself.

Imagine today that the world
you see is the world that
is of your own making.

What will you create today?
How will you be?
What will you say and
how will you respond?

Let love guide your way.
Let the miracle of life
constantly inspire you.
See the world as blessed,
and creation as a blessing.
See all behaviours as expressions
OF love or as cries FOR love.

Fill every moment and event
with all the love you can today.

DAY 292

God, how would you have me be in the world today?

Be the surprise of a warm day
    in the middle of winter –
bright sun and hardly a cloud in the sky.

Imagine the joy that would bring –
    a sign offering the hope of spring.
Imagine people stepping out to enjoy
    the welcome warmth and light.

Be a place of welcoming warmth
    filled with beauty and gracious light.
Be a place of hope today,
    and a source of inspiration,
encouragement, and support.

Where you see darkness and coldness,
    embrace them with the light of love
and the warmth of compassion.
    Embrace the pain with your thoughts
and prayers.

When you see someone hurting,
    soothe them with words
that encourage hope to rise
    and healing to begin.

Today, be the love and light
    of God.
Wherever you go,
    whatever you say and do,
be the warm-day-in-winter surprise.

EVENING REFLECTION

I attended two meetings today, and in each one there were moments of honest tension and concern. I was aware that I had opportunities to add a ray of light and some warmth to the proceedings that might be able to cut through the cold breeze that was blowing in the room. I was in a position to speak, and I did.

The guidance helped me to not get caught up in the coldness. I thought I would add light and warmth by providing a bit of comic relief. I don't consider myself to be funny but I love humour and recognize its power to transform energy. The humorous story I offered diffused the tension to the extent that the people in the room could hear each other better, accept our differing views, and move on to other matters that needed our consideration.

A few people came to me afterward and said my timing had been perfect and my story what the moment of tension needed. It wasn't that I carried the guidance's image with me every moment of this day, as I was working alone for much it. But when it was needed, the guidance provided a great image to work with.

How did the guidance serve you today?

DAY 293

God, how can I be of service today?

Make peace
   with the things you've done
and with what you've left undone.

Concentrate on what is before you
   NOW
      and offer yourself to it
      in service to the world
      and life itself.

Trust that your past has unfolded
   as it has for divine reasons,
and that things left undone
     or not pursued
were, simply put,
meant for others.

You cannot do all the things that
   come to you in the form of ideas...
      they are as plentiful as grains of sand.
      Know that you are doing
         what you are meant to do.

As for today's tasks –
   do them to the best of your ability.
     Each is a step in the direction
of your destiny.

Each small act you perform
   contributes to the greater unfolding.

     Keep going.
  You are in the right place,
    right now,
in this present moment.

EVENING REFLECTION

Today I came across a company that was doing something I had the idea to do ten years ago. In fact, I had written about it when I worked as editor-in-chief for a magazine. It involves a physical exercise workout where I take a traditional machine like a bike, or a glider, or a treadmill, and I expand its use. In my case, I took a stationary bike and developed a way to do specific muscle isolations while riding and boogying down to some great music.

When I read up on this company, I was surprised to learn that two women had turned the idea into a business that had been going for about ten years – which put its beginning at about the same time I came up with the same idea! It reminded me that ideas belong to all of us. They are floating in the atmosphere, so to speak, ready to be picked up and used by those with the vision and commitment to actually Do It.

Have you ever had that experience? Of someone actualizing "your" idea?

Ideas belong to the human community. Whoever engages their inspirational antennae to grab or receive an idea and goes with it profits from it. My idea has brought great satisfaction to my personal workouts, and the same idea turned into a business has brought joy to many others.

Now I doubt any of us can do something with all the good ideas that come into our heads, but when we see our ideas turned into successful businesses by someone else, it should remind us that we are not the only ones who have those ideas...and if we don't do something with them, someone else is bound to at some point.

Whatever ideas you have – if they are really strong, DO SOMETHING! Find out how to do them, get help doing them – or someone else will do them for you.

That being said, I have made peace. And you?

DAY 294

God, how can I be more loving today?

Be ready to help.

To be ready is to stay sensitive.
Then you will know
    what to do.
    To help is to add to
a being's ease of living,
    whether human or non-human.

    Lift a burden,
even if only for a moment.
Offer words of
    affirmation, kindness, and hope.

    Help with a chore,
supply a smile, or offer nourishment.

Today, be helpful by
    staying mindful and sensitive,
noticing who or what may be
    in need of your time,
kindness, wisdom, and willingness.
    Offer those things with compassion
and grace.

DAY 295

God, how may I be of service? How can I be more loving today?

Today, rest...
    Rest your being.
        Rest your soul.

        Take deep breaths
    and exhale slowly.
    Even if you are under
pressure and have deadlines
to meet,
find a way
    to be alone for a few
        precious minutes.

    Remember that you are of spirit.
    Remember you are a
    divine being.

    Remember to love others
as you are loved by me.
    Be kind and gracious.
    Shine your light.
You can do all of this by
    resting today
        in my gentle
            care.

EVENING REFLECTION

To be able to rest while being busy is a good trick, for sure. But it can be done.

To achieve rest in the midst of busyness, we must pay attention to the details. Though we usually breathe automatically, we can also pay attention to our breath and control it. We can inhale deeply and exhale slowly and release any tension that may be hiding in your shoulders, for instance. We can exhale hard and fast and get rid of an unwanted odour. Furthermore, we can scan our bodies for the anxieties, frustrations, or worries that we hold in the moment. These may be hiding out in the shadows and expressed in a certain head tilt, body posture, or unconscious movement (such as finger tapping). Then we can take a deep breath and, as best we can, let these unwanteds go as we exhale. Allow that small pause between inhale and exhale to become a place where we rest and give it all to God. Of course, letting go is not always easy, but even if we do it for just a few moments, it will pay dividends.

Living in a relaxed, restful manner is a challenge, especially when we are involved in the chaos and busyness of the world. But remembering to relax and rest while carrying out our tasks and duties goes a long way in helping us to achieve just that.

How was the rest of your day?

DAY 296

God, what would you have me say and do today?

Today...
   be your own inspiration.

Take stock of your life
and all the good things you have
done and accomplished.

Remember wise decisions
you have made
   and lessons you have
learned from the unwise ones.

Take time to appreciate yourself
and how you have evolved as a
   child of the universe –
as a son or daughter of God.

Let the wonder of your life
fill you with gratitude and humility.
   Be amazed at your journey
and let it fill you with awe.

Let the miracle of it all
inspire you to live today with joy
   and gratitude...
for YOU!

DAY 297

God, what would you have me say and do today?

Supervise yourself.
   Be your own coach today.

Watch yourself
   and stay aware of what
      you are doing.

Silently remind yourself
   to be beautiful,
loving, kind, courteous,
   gracious, gentle, caring...

Be a good listener today,
   and listen to guidance
      and wisdom coming through
         for yourself as well.

Hear yourself speak
   and adjust your tones to
      honour the divine light
         coming through you.

Watch your actions and mannerisms
   and adjust them, if need be,
      to reflect compassion and gentleness.

Supervise and coach yourself today,
   and be the beautiful soul you are.

EVENING REFLECTION

It is an interesting exercise to actively coach and supervise ourselves, to stay so aware of ourselves in the moment that we almost feel like two people inside one body – one doing, and one watching the doer.

Many actors use this skill when performing. That is, they pour themselves into a role, but remain aware enough to control the character they are portraying. On the stage of our real lives, sometimes we "catch" ourselves being a certain way. We may then find ourselves apologizing for not having realized how we were sounding or acting until the deed was done.

That is why today's guidance is important, and one that I should perhaps refer to often. As we practice mindfulness, we achieve more self-mastery – one small step at a time, moment by moment.

So how did you do with this one today?

DAY 298

God, how would you have me be in the world today?

Have strong faith today.

Faith in what?

Faith that I am...
and that I am for you...
and that I love you...
and that I am always with you.

Faith that I will protect
your spirit
no matter what transpires in
the world or what happens to your body.

In the face of tragedy,
catastrophe, and the worst of
human actions,
remain certain of my love
and care for you.

Remember you can express beauty,
offer kindness,
unfold acts of love,
and forge friendships and bonds.

Do one of these things today...

EVENING REFLECTION

Today I received a phone call from a friend going through a tough time. During the course of our conversation he mentioned he didn't have much faith in a positive outcome and that he felt distant from people and, especially, from God.

I remembered the guidance and let him know he could hook on to my faith for a while. He said that was why he had called – he knew he could talk to me and feel more hopeful because of my strong faith. I told him I had done the same thing many times in my life – talked to people I knew were strong of faith at a time when mine was weak.

Jesus reminded us of the power of faith when he told us that faith the size of a mustard seed could move mountains. Still, there are times when we need to "borrow" faith from others until ours is strong again. Being around the energy of another with strong faith – even via the telephone – can give us a foothold to use to climb back up to higher faithful ground.

How did you do with your faith today?

DAY 299

**God, what would you have me say and do today?
How would you have me be in the world?**

Be grounded today.
  Sink your soul into the
depths of divinity.
  Take time to centre your being
in divine love.

  Feel your life purpose and
consciously live in it today.

  Speak and act from the
depths of your wisdom and experience.

  Do not hurry today.
Be settled in your being and patient
with the flow of the day.

  Be a caring listener.

  Walk slowly
and feel your feet hitting the ground.
Yes, you are walking on the earth.

  Speak with care and hear yourself.
Keep kindness in the tone of your voice.

  Eat with appreciation.
Taste and savour each bite.

Live with gratitude for everything.

  Be rooted in goodness
and let all you say and do
have the strength of love.

DAY 300

God, how may I be of service today?

As you go through your day,
be prepared to serve others
  by offering your time and presence.

Affirm those who call upon you.
Acknowledge their wisdom and insight.
  Hold their challenges
with care and gentleness.

Listen with love.

Yes, open your heart today
if others call upon you,
  yet be attentive to your
own work, as it too serves all.

Be joyful as you work and serve,
  and be grateful for
your skills and talents.

Today you serve the Great Work,
  even as the Great Work
serves you.

DAY 301

God, what would you have me say and do today?

Let today be a quiet day.

Let silence bathe you in its peace.
    Listen to the whispers of your soul.

In this quietness, sense
    my soundless presence.

Feel its noiseless love embrace you
    and bless you.

Breathe in the stillness,
    and centre yourself in
the low hum of its creative powers.

Move, speak, and act from this
    place of quiet today,
no matter the noise around you.

You can carry this quiet into any space.
    You can be this quiet...

Today,
    you are this quiet.

Can you hear it yet?

EVENING REFLECTION

Today was very successful. Very. I did turn my day into a beautiful exercise in quiet.

Until...

Yes, that *until* can do it every time.

My *until* happened at about 10:00 p.m. If I had gone to bed, I would have lived a near-perfect execution of today's beautiful guidance. But someone close to me came by and was not in a good mood. They eventually drew me into a heated debate (or, better, I allowed it).

I fell hard out of my quiet zone.

Afterward – after the apologies – I realized I had once again been thwarted in my effort to perfectly follow the guidance. I am happy, though, to remember that our progress in life is not predicated on perfection but intention. As the saying goes, progress, not perfection.

And you? What happened in your quiet day?

DAY 302

God, how would you have me be in the world today? What would you have me say and do?

Do not try to be anything today.
Just be.

Meld with the day and all
that unfolds.

Let all things be what they are
without trying to change them
or mould them to your liking.

Accept things as they are.
Relax...and be alive.

Enjoy the day
with all your senses.

Be aware of your breath
and accept with joy and gratitude
the precious gift of your life.

Look upon the day and marvel
quietly that you are living it.

Today, fit into the tapestry
of creation and enjoy just being.

EVENING REFLECTION

Today was a beautiful exercise in feeling intertwined with our natural environment – earth to sky to limitless cosmos. It was an exercise in fitting in, rather than looking for ways to stand out.

So much of our time is spent trying to transcend the human-made classifications and labels that separate us from the earth and all other creatures. However, the guidance today is about the equality of all creation. Everything is equal to everything else.

Allowing ourselves to accept this truth is to allow rest. If we believe we are equal, we live without feeling the need to live up to anything or prove anything to anybody. Our birth is our proof of worthiness! We can relax and witness the beauty, awe, and wonder of creation and existence.

I will come back to this guidance many times, I'm sure.

How did you do with just being today?

DAY 303

God, what would you have me say and do today?

Stand with someone in need today,
   in spirit if not in person.

     Think of someone
  who is in need
and be with them.

Pray for them throughout the day –
   send them love, supportive thoughts,
     and good wishes.

If it is someone you know, call them,
   if it feels right, and let them know
     you are thinking about them.

If it is someone recovering from a
   recent illness, or someone in jail,
     perhaps pay them a visit.

     We all need support at times –
  someone to stand with us,
show up for us, and believe in us.

Today, be that someone
   and add to the healing
     and restoration of the world.

DAY 304

God, what would you have me say and do today?

Let your day revolve around camaraderie...
   that feeling of friendship
     and mutual trust engendered
      by shared experience.
     Think of the people
   you share time and space with
and extend to them today a special dose of
   care through your words and actions.
     Demonstrate your understanding of
   their experiences and challenges
and share your compassion and encouragement.

Extend this camaraderie even to those
you encounter in passing:
   give a nod of the head to an overheard
     conversation,
   offer a smile of understanding to someone
     while waiting in a long line,
   wave someone into your lane in heavy traffic.
There are countless ways to extend
and experience camaraderie.

How will you do that today?

DAY 305

God, what would you have me say, do, or be like today?

Today,
    take stock of how you live,
        and review the purpose
            of your life.

What fuels your volition?
    What gives you the
        energy to pursue
            your life purpose?

How does your purpose
    line up with your actions?

Where could you focus more
    energy to increase the
        power and effect
            of your life purpose?

What commitment can you make
    or remake today that will
        affirm and refresh your
            direction and desires?

    Make your commitment with
resolve, humility,
and the power of intention.

DAY 306

God, how would you have me be in the world today?

    Be still.
    Be stillness.

Picture yourself as
a place of rest and repose.

Envision yourself as deep water
    in a still lake,
        or as divinity
    resting within itself.

Carry this stillness with you
throughout your day.
    Move and speak from this
    deeply centred place.
        Let even the resonance of your
        voice embrace the sound of peace.

Enacting this vision through
the powers of your imagination and intention,
    you will notice rich and awesome
    subtleties that the din of life has obscured.
        You will receive insight, and gain
        understanding on a deeper level.
    You will see and hear with more sensitivity.
    You will receive and comprehend guidance
    that is more nuanced.

Be alert to my voice within you
as you may be guided to offer
    an encouraging word
    or a caring act.

Or you may simply be a peaceful
presence wherever you are –
    a blessing for those
    who may have need to
        rest in peace
        today.

DAY 307

God, how may I be of service today?

Take time
  to perform some small action
    that may make a
      difference in someone's
      day.
It could be making
  a cup of tea for a busy
    family member,
  buying lunch for a co-worker
    who is overloaded with work,
  or finding the perfect
    joke to tell someone
      who could use a good laugh.
Keep your awareness
    open to serving in this
    way and you will
  know what to do and for whom.
The beauty of this is that
  you will feel joy
    when you offer
      unexpected kindness.

DAY 308

God, how can I be more loving today?

Don't hold back.

When an opportunity presents itself
for you to express love, do so without
reservation or condition.

  Don't hold back.

Remember that all creation
  is formed from the same essence –
divine love.

Remember to see yourself
  when you look at
another person.

Remember that what you
  say and do to another,
you say and do to yourself.

    Today,
  don't hold back.
Don't hold back your love.

As you love,
  your own reservoir
    will be filled
  by the One who
pours out love onto and into
all of creation itself.

DAY 309

God, what would you have me say, do, or be like today?

Be the person you really want to be –
that person you imagine and hold
   close to your heart.

That person has nothing to do
   with your income, gender, race, or culture.
That person has everything to do
   with how you treat others,
   even with your thoughts.
That person has to do with your actions.

You are already
   familiar with that person.
Today, let go of whatever holds you back
   from being that person.
Let go of that which makes you
   less than you want to be.

Today,
   be Light Shining.
   Be Love That Liberates.
   Be Hope That Inspires.
   Be the person you really are –
the person who blesses with tenderness,
the person who heals with kindness,
the person whose faith allows miracles to happen,
the person whose joy of being gives life to life.

EVENING REFLECTION

Many people are afraid to be who they really want to be. They are afraid of failure and so never "go for it." However, this guidance directs our attention toward how we are in the world as our everyday selves – the ways we move and flow and express our being.

There are people who love to hate, and that is how they want to be. They may even believe they have a duty to hate. They are most likely not reading this book. Those who are have already committed to growing in love. I found that living today's guidance was about staying connected to my heart and imagination, just like it said. The person we imagine we can be – we CAN be. If it were not so, we wouldn't be able to imagine it.

But to make miracles happen?

Yes.

A miracle does not have to be of the raising-of-the-dead variety. Bringing joy into someone's day, making someone smile, lighting a spark of hope in someone's darkened heart are all miracles. We may not think so at first, but these small acts can change lives, if only for a short time. They may also be seeds that fall on fertile soil, germinate, and become part of the reason a life is transformed.

DAY 310

God, how may I be of service today?

Respect all you encounter today.

Include people, animals, insects,
    and the rest of nature
        in your respectful regard.

Respectfulness means considering another,
    avoiding harm to another,
        seeing another as equally deserving.

This takes commitment
    to awakening to and being aware of
        divinity in everything.

If you can do this today,
    you will be a source of
        peace and joy for others...
            an instrument of healing and
            compassion for all nature,
        and a true
friend of creation.

Today, be respectful,
    and enjoy the feeling
        within you.

DAY 311

God, how would you have me be in the world today?

Be the constant
amidst the chaos.

Be solid ground
for others to stand on.

Be sturdy
that others can lean on you and feel held.

As the winds of time swirl about the day,
be steady –
rock solid.

Express your belief in the strength
and triumph of my care,
no matter the struggles, pains, challenges,
or outcomes.
Let it be the source of your presence.

Let the light within be your
ground of being today
and many will be helped
by your constancy.

DAY 312

God, what would you have me say or do today?

Do something today that makes
    another person's day easier...
something that lightens a load
    or takes a little of the pressure off.

Say something hilarious that
    brightens someone's moment.
Reaching out in an unexpected way
    may be the thing
        that makes a big difference.

Remind someone how incredible he or she is.

Let someone know how they have
    inspired you or been of help to you –
someone who may not be aware of his or her
    gift to you.

Champion someone and let them know
you think that they are
    the *cat's meow*,
        the *bee's knees*...
    or whatever
cool idiom works for you.
But tell them.

Today,
    acknowledge someone's gifts and talents.
Let them know you appreciate
what they do.

Yes, today
    have someone's back,
    lighten someone's burden,
champion someone.

In fact,
    be a cheerleader for all souls today.

DAY 313

God, what would you have me be like in the world today?

Be open and receptive to everything that fosters
growth.

That means being open to critique and criticism.

You will notice your ego react to opposition.
This guidance is about transcending the boundaries your ego is attempting to defend so that you
can become more of what you already are –

    genius and blessing.

If critique or criticism comes your way today
welcome it as a divine message
meant to guide you.

    Others see what you do not see,
    or do not want to see.

The hardest part will be to
    appreciate and thank anyone
        who cares enough to have
    the courage to speak up.

Appreciate even those who
speak out of envy or dislike.
Their truth may be valid
    even if the motivation is
        less than optimum.

    Thank them, all of them.
    And thank me for sending them.

EVENING REFLECTION

I am creating a project that is close to my heart. I am more sensitive about the cracks in it than I am about other things. I have been allowing a few people sneak peeks, and they are chiming in.

Today's guidance is a reminder that other people, especially those who have similar talents, have insights different from our own – useful ideas that may not have occurred to us. Though it might be great to be amazing at everything and have no need of revision, that is not usually the case. Coaches, teachers, and mentors all serve in helping to make us better at being what we are being.

We should be genuinely grateful to those who step up to give feedback when called upon. And we should thank them, no matter what is offered. To make another person feel comfortable critiquing "our baby," even if we feel uncomfortable, takes will and courage and a big heart. We must push our ego aside and receive love in the form of correction, advice, or insight from another's perspective and genius.

The more we listen, the more we serve. God can and does speak to us through others.

DAY 314

God, what would you have me say, do, or be like today?

Let everything you say drip
   with love's
      compassion, care,
         courtesy, kindness,
     and respect.

Today,
   see the best
     in others,
       even if they
         show you otherwise.
    Be open and
  welcoming,
allowing yourself
   to be a safe place
     for others to
      come to.
    Listen as if
   listening is your
greatest gift...
   and then respond
     with a warm heart
    full of encouragement,
support, and understanding.

Breath quietly and evenly
   today, as you become the
     embodiment
      of love.
     Yes, you.

Are you ready?

DAY 315

God, what would you have me say and do today? How may I be of service?

Don't take yourself
so seriously!
   Go about your day
and be happy.
   Do your work and
remember that you are part of
the Great Work.
   Allow yourself enjoyment,
remembering your earthly life is
finite.

Let this reality encourage you
   to savour the day.
Let each moment and encounter
be precious and special.

No matter what you may accomplish today,
   you need humility
     to be of service.
So embrace it.

No matter who you are, you can
   be kind and gracious
and regard every person
   as you would wish to be regarded.

Today,
   do not take yourself so seriously,
and regard others with respect.

DAY 316

God, how may I be more loving today?

Make this a No Complaints day.
Whatever comes up, take it
   in stride,
as if it is the most natural
of occurrences.
Just breathe and accept
   with faith and trust
that your life is unfolding
as it should.

If something unexpected and surprising
   challenges or confronts you,
     give it to me.
       Ask for wisdom
       and trust my guidance.
   Look for a lesson to be learned,
   or an opportunity to extend
love and compassion in some way.

But no matter what transpires –
   no matter how annoying, or frustrating,
   or inconvenient things may be –
     do not complain.
     Not today.
   In fact, say, *Thank you*
   for all that you experience.
No exceptions.
None.
Not today.
This is a No Complaints day.
Okay?

DAY 317

God, what would you have me say, do, or be like
today?

Imagine awakening to a misty morning,
    breathing in the fresh, cool air
    and rousing your senses.

Take in this image
and let the words you speak today
be refreshing and invigorating,
supportive and encouraging.

Be motivated by your awakened
appreciation of being alive.

Give attention to your mind,
    body, and spirit.
Breathe in fresh inspiration for your mind,
    exercise your body,
and provide silence for your soul.

Honour the gift of this new day,
then give back to the
world the refreshing beauty of
    all you say, all you do,
and all you are.

DAY 318

God, what would you have me say and do today?

Listen to your own genius today,
    for you have your own
in your own way.
    Listen to truth
from inside your soul
    for what it knows
can keep you whole.

There are many people who
    know many things,
but your truth is brought to you
    by your own life experience.
Let your soul speak –
    and listen well –
for your soul is connected to
    wisdom's well.

Within this day's rhymes
    and rhythms,
find time to
    hear the silent soundings
    coming through and guiding you
in what to say and what to do.

At the end of the day,
    pause and take stock
of all the wisdom and guidance
    you have received,
and thank me for loving you
    and sending a song
just right
    for you to sing.

DAY 319

God, what would you have me say or do today?

Bring peace,
    make peace,
    and keep the peace.
Along with love and joy,
peace holds the universe together.

Start with your breathing.
    Let go of
        tension, anxiety, or animosity.
    Breathe in peace,
        breathe out peace.

Let your breath carry
    the energy of peace
and let peaceful thoughts inform
your actions today.
    Let your movements transmit the
    energy of peace.

    Let this peace
flow through you like a river
and spill over the banks
of your being.

    Today, be peace on earth
        and allow nothing to
            stop its spread
                into the world.

DAY 320

God, what would you have me say, do, or be like today?

Today,
look at your personal problems, challenges, and
issues.
    Own them and own up to them.

Place each one into a larger context.

    What context?

My context.

Anything you place within my loving
divine energy
will be met with my compassion and wisdom.

Pray your challenges into my care.
Keep your prayers honest
and your inner eyes open
to the larger framework and perspective.

Sense my guidance.
Let inspiration find you.

As you change the context, feel your fear lessen
and your hope increase.

Have faith and hold on – for you are not alone.

EVENING REFLECTION

This guidance reminds us to step back and examine
our challenges within a larger context. When we do
this, the intensity of our challenges somehow shrinks
and we feel less stressed. Placing our biggest challenges into a divine container can give us hope that
we actually can come through our ordeals intact. As
we trust Spirit, we can move from fear to faith, from
worry to wonder, from frustration to inspiration.

It may take time to work out our biggest challenges,
but we will always have company on the journey –
divine company.

DAY 321

God, what would you have me be like today?

Where would you like to grow?
Where would you like to improve?

The journey of life
   has taken you many
      places...
You have had many experiences
and have learned and grown much.
   But now –
     Who and what inspires you?
Even as you are beautiful and perfect,
   you can still become...
Do not settle for coasting on
   who you are or have been.
     Your "better" makes the
       universe better...
      Every improvement improves
   our world.
It is your gift back to life.

EVENING REFLECTION

There are countless ways to live life. There are countless perspectives on how to see it and understand it. The common lenses we look at life through include gender, race, nationality, and culture, among others. These lenses are placed upon us fairly early. But they can be swapped out for others – and the boxes we are locked in can be transcended as we expand our souls.

Personal growth is an exciting adventure that we can consciously engage in all our lives. Some people stop growing, satisfied with who they are and the way they are. But others, while happy with who and what they are, desire to grow. They want to see where the growth of their soul can take them.

We can change careers several times in a lifetime. We can learn a new skill at any time. Age cannot limit us – we only limit ourselves. People have received advanced degrees at advanced ages (and at precociously early ages as well).

We can also grow to amazing levels of love and spiritual advancement.

The question is, who do you want to be? Are you willing to do the work, or find out how to become that being, or move toward that expression of yourself?

Do you still have a dream living in the internal vision of YOU?

When I was in a state of doubt, unsure of myself or wondering how things would go, my minister father would tell me, with a smile on his face and joy in his voice, "Just keep on living...and see what happens!"

What a great and inspiring call to life!

DAY 322

God, what would you have me say or do today?

Today,
identify something you want to change about
yourself.
Then begin the process of change.

Change what?
You decide.
But change something.

Envision how you might be when this change is
complete.
Find out how to get there if you do not already
know.

Tell someone what you are thinking,
to hear how it sounds.
    Or keep it to yourself
and allow the idea to develop inside.

Read about it.
Research it.
Perhaps find a picture that expresses the change
And put it up somewhere you can see it.
    Find a theme song to inspire you.
        Play it – often!

Celebrate your decision to change.
And just begin.

And tomorrow, and the next day, and the next...
remember this day –
the day you decided
to change.

DAY 323

God, what would you have me say, do, or be like today?

    Be attentive
to the preciousness of life.

You will not have to look hard,
        for precious moments occur
during the most ordinary days.

Today, notice subtle looks
    of grace and gratitude,
the slight smiles of hopeful souls,
        the innocence of children at play.

Watch for someone's act of kindness,
    another's silent nod of affirmation to a total
stranger,
actions that express the beauty of being human.

They happen in the blink of an eye.
    Don't miss them. Look for them.
Let them affect you – get to you.

Today, amidst the worst of the daily news,
    see your best.
See what makes humanity
– you –
so precious to me,
    because...
        you are.

EVENING REFLECTION

My wife woke me early this morning with the news that a deer, a buck that frequented our property, was in distress and seemingly stuck in our backyard fence. By the time I got downstairs I found it lying on its side unable to get up, struggling for breath, and rolling its eyes and mooing every so often. The sound was recognizable in any living creature. It was the sound of suffering.

We called animal services and a park ranger came to assess the situation. He could see nothing externally wrong with the animal we had come to call "Bucky." He summoned another ranger and together they tried to help the deer stand up, with no success. They measured its antlers and surmised that the animal was old...and was dying. They said that, as far as they could tell, it was just the deer's time.

The rangers told us that it was unusual for a deer to be in such a condition in someone's yard, and that if it had been coming as often as we said, then it seemed it had, for some reason, chosen our property on which to die. They decided it was best to put the buck out of its misery since it was clearly suffering and unresponsive to the help being offered.

After the rangers left, my wife and I spent some time honouring the blessings we had received because of Bucky, who would often come and stay all day. We wondered where he went at night. We wondered why he chose us. He would sit in one of three areas throughout the day, all of which were perfect spots to view us without being seen by neighbours. He would stare at us in the house, washing dishes or working in the office. Once, when we were in our backyard Jacuzzi, he walked right past us, pooping as he strode by. We took that as a sign of endearment and acceptance on Bucky's part. At least that's what we decided to think.

We are left with the legacy of having experienced this deer up close for two years and being the witnesses of its death. We are honoured, saddened, and ultimately blessed, because Bucky was a great teacher for us. He showed us daily what peace looks like. He showed us what sitting meditation looks like, what it is to be completely relaxed, and even what it looks like to chew your food – and just chew your food! He showed us what it looks like to simply observe – to just look and see. Bucky was a priest, and a great one at that. He was a living word of God and a great example of living in the present moment. He was a prayer and an answered prayer at the same time, and a great teacher of meditation.

Bucky was precious. We loved Bucky and I think he sensed that. Perhaps it is one reason he stayed. At least that is what we have decided to think.

DAY 324

God, how may I be of service? What would you have me say, do, or be like in the world? How can I be more loving today?

Is this the day?

Is this the day to start doing
what you find difficult to do?

Or is this the day to stop doing
what you probably wanted to stop doing
a long time ago?

Is this the day you open to a
new way for yourself?

Perhaps this is the day
to make a new commitment to:
    continue spiritual growth
    and development,
      love unconditionally,
        serve someone in need,
      express love in a new way,
    pray more for the world,
listen deeply for guidance and direction.

Perhaps this is the day
    you go
      even
          d
          e
          e
          p
          e
          r.

DAY 325

God, what would you have me say or do today?

Recall a dream you've had recently.
Contemplate what it means to you.

    A dream is a window into your soul
    and your subconscious mind.

    What is this dream telling you?
    What is it telling you about you?

The dreams you remember are often about things
you are ready to deal with.

    Are you ready?

If not, what do you need
to become ready?
Ask me for what you need.

And then, if you are ready,
do one thing
that your dream speaks to you about.

    What will that be?
    What will you do today?

DAY 326

God, how may I be of service today?

Let your actions show you are
committed to caring for
and sustaining the life and welfare
 of the planet.

The earth is strong and fragile,
always seeking balance and harmony.
The earth is alive and intelligent.
 Earth can take only so much abuse.

I have given the earth
to provide for you food, air, water,
and shelter.

 But can the earth rely on you?

Think of something you can do today
that will demonstrate your
awareness and concern
 for the earth's need for care.

What to do?

There are countless choices,
from praying, to participating
in projects designed to spread awareness,
 to making hard individual choices that serve to
sustain the earth.

Today, love your world...
 and show it.

DAY 327

God, what would you have me say or do today?

Today,
 practice loving speech
  and deep listening.

Let every word you speak
 be loving.

Listen deeply and patiently
 so that you hear beneath
  the words that are said...
 and are able to respond
with sensitivity and compassion.

Take your time.
 Do not rush or allow yourself
  to be hurried into speaking.

Take a deep breath before speaking.
 Receive calm and grace.
Let your words be filled with them.

You will affect many
 in a positive way
  and be a wonderful
 blessing today.

DAY 328

God, what would you have me say, do, or be like today?

Be confident in your body today.
　　By doing so, you uplift and influence others.

Do your best.
Remember that confidence comes from
appreciating the priceless gift of having a body.

If you notice yourself looking downward
while talking to others, lift your eyes.
Let them shine with love.

Stay relaxed and comfortable.
Be natural and have an easy manner.

Be a humble but powerful
force of goodness, love, light, and peace.

Let your beauty and being
demonstrate divine love.

And remember that I live in your body too.

DAY 329

God, what would you have me be like in the world today?

Patiently bear suffering today.

Whatever troubles you,
　　let it be what it is.
　　Accept it, don't fight it.
and turn the situation over to me.

Also receive grace.
Remind yourself that
　　　life is filled
　　　with ups and downs,
　　joy and pain.
And remember that trouble doesn't last.

When you cannot change things and must endure,
then remember I am with you.

So...
Hold on.
　　Hold on.
　　　Don't give up on yourself.
　　Keep the faith
and carry on.

EVENING REFLECTION

The universe hears us when we speak.

Soon after receiving this day's guidance, I went to see a musical in which some friends of mine were performing. All seats in the theatre were unreserved but the theatre sections were colour-coded on the ticket. I was the first person inside and took a seat on the aisle. I wanted to sit away from others so I could really concentrate on the show, as I had not seen my friends perform in a long while. I thought I had found the perfect seat.

Eventually a woman approached me. She inquired if the section I was in might be her section as well. I looked at her ticket and confirmed that it was. She asked if someone was with me. I said no...and she promptly sat right next to me even though there were still many empty seats in our row. She immediately began talking my ear off. I tried to be polite even as I engaged as little as possible, glancing in her direction only occasionally while trying to be obvious about concentrating on the pre-show happenings. I also used a flat voice that I hoped would convey my lack of interest in conversing. She did not get the hint. She even sat forward in her seat so she could turn and look me square in the face!

It was then that I realized I had entered my guidance and was experiencing...suffering! I laughed to myself at the brilliance of how life finds ways to test us when we least expect it or cannot ignore it.

The woman finally stopped talking when the show began but commented after every musical number. I realized she was alone and wanted connection, but I was not on that page. I did my best to be courteous and still allow myself the space I desired. At the intermission I made the decision to change seats and was able to enjoy the second half of the show in peace. However, she found me after the show as I was speaking with one of the performers. "What happened to you?" she exclaimed. I simply told her that I wanted to see the second half from a different vantage point.

Now of course this short-course form of suffering is not the same as a truly difficult and trying situation that one cannot escape from easily or anytime soon. Still, it was a glimpse of suffering, and a reminder of the grace it may take to put up with difficult circumstances while figuring out how to take care of oneself as well.

How did I do? I lasted through to intermission today. But life rarely gives us intermissions.

How did your day play out?

DAY 330

God, what would you have me say, do, or be like
today?

Be the calm
in the middle of the storm.

Be silent sanctuary for others
within the busyness of the day –
    open and welcoming,
    kind and courteous,
    an oasis of refreshment and rest.

Be the breath of fresh air
in an otherwise turbulent day
swirling with metaphorical haze and dust.

Learn a short, hilarious new joke
    or an engaging riddle.
Keep an inspiring quote at hand.
Be ready to share them.

Be ready to be a listening ear
and truly hear another.

And if need be,
be still with someone
who desires not to talk or be talked to,
but who needs a loving, supportive presence...
the calm
in the middle of the storm.

Are you willing to be this today?

DAY 331

God, how would you have me be in the world
today?

Imagine you are a human being
    with all the qualities
        that make the world a better place
    for all its inhabitants.

    Hold this image in your mind
and carry it with you throughout your day.
Look out through
    its eyes,
        speak with its voice,
    and communicate its essence.

The world is affected by every
    thought and action,
        no matter how subtle,
    no matter who notices...or not.

Whatever you do today
is incorporated into creation
and its ongoing evolution.

Be strong in your effort today.
    It matters.
And you matter –
    as a powerful source of
        change in the world.

DAY 332

God, how may I be of service today?

Make a commitment to
be of service today.
Stay mindful and aware
of your thoughts and feelings.
Remember that serving
with integrity, humility, and love
is of great value.
Keep yourself aligned with being
humble and loving.
A powerful synergy will allow you to be
a beacon of willingness.
You will attract those whom
you are to serve.
You will know who they are when they show up,
and I will guide you.
Know that it is
an honour and a privilege
to be of service
to another.

Are you willing to be of service today?

EVENING REFLECTION

As of this writing I am visiting my mother for a few days. The day after I arrived, she cut her hand opening a can of green beans. She didn't want to go to the clinic – she wanted to finish cooking a special family meal. So I patched her up. The next morning, I took her to a nearby clinic. There were several people in line in front of us and my mother asked me if I wanted to wait. I let her know I had nothing better to do than make sure her wound was cared for, and we ended up spending half the day there, mostly waiting. The nurse practitioner gave my mother a tetanus shot, some antibiotics, and pain medication, and showed us how to change the dressing.

My mother later thanked me for my patience. Patience was the appropriate word for the day, since she was a...patient! (Did you see that one coming?) My mother talked to me about the lack of patience she knew some others would have had in the same situation and thanked me again.

Patience may come naturally for some, but it is a learned skill for others, as I have experienced. It has to do with letting go of the need for control and having faith that things will work out in their own divine time. When we are truly patient, our stress lessens and our feelings of disappointment when things don't happen according to our desired timetable are less intense. One of my favorite sermons that my dad preached was on patience. I heard it first as a young boy and had the pleasure of hearing him share it a few more times during his ministry. I guess, on some level, he and God knew I needed to hear this lesson early on and often!

How are you with this virtue? How did you serve today?

DAY 333

God, how can I be more loving today?

You'll know how.
> Just keep the question in mind
>> and the way will be revealed.
>> Asking the question
> will reveal the answer.

Just keep asking.

The real question is...
> Will you do what
> you are asked to do?

Love is a verb
> as well as a feeling.
>> It demands action and effort.

Being more loving makes
> the world a better place – instantly.
>> Love is the reason
>>> the universe exists,
>> and being loving allows us to
> resonate with its essence.

Today, keep asking the question,
> and upon knowing the answer...
>> love.

EVENING REFLECTION

Today was a talking day. What I mean is, I needed to listen – for some hours – as a friend told me his story. I knew he respected me as well as my work, and he wanted me to know what he was doing, especially since it had been some time since we'd had a heart-to-heart. Although I had tentatively planned a couple of other activities, I rescheduled them, sensing that the most loving thing to do would be to give my friend this time.

Ultimately, it was a good thing. Listening and asking questions, letting another hear back what they are communicating to you, and giving loving feedback all make for a rich exchange of time and heart. They are Holy Spirit times, when hearts and minds communicate and divine work gets done. We both came away from that time of sharing knowing each other better (though I hardly spoke compared to my friend's outpouring!). I learned much about listening, and my friend learned I can be a trusted ear.

It would not work for me to engage in this kind of exchange on a daily basis. But for this day it was perfectly timed. And it was an opportunity to live and experience the guidance, which proved helpful to a good friend. And for that, I am grateful.

Were you more loving today? How? If not, why?

DAY 334

God, what would you have me say and do today?

Let your love show.

Let those you love hear about it today.
Say it directly.
Yes – say, *I love you.*
Then say it again in other ways
that can be felt
beneath every word you speak to them.

Let them feel it
in your voice,
let them see it in your eyes.
Keep letting your love show
all day.

Let it flow naturally from your heart;
it will regulate itself and not
overwhelm,
and it will guide you in
what to say or do
for others.

Be open to love's power,
   its surprises and divine magic,
   its joy in being known,
     its divine kiss
     that bestows blessing,
   creates healing,
   strengthens souls,
and makes whole.

This was a beautiful reminder to let people know we love them. And it was fun. It was fun to see what I could do to communicate love without saying the words, and without being overt or feeling like an actor on stage acting out love in broad strokes. The most intriguing part of the guidance for me was the sentence about love regulating itself so that it does not overwhelm. I found that it did just that – regulate itself – although at first the concept felt strange. But as water flow is regulated by a faucet, love's outward flow is governed by the heart, which knows we cannot go around being demonstrative and effusive all the time. I found that I knew when and how to say what. I also felt my actions being guided in the moment, regulated by love itself and the wisdom inherent in it.

What was your experience with today's guidance?

DAY 335

God, how may I be of service today?

Be present for someone encountering a
challenge.
If you cannot physically be with the person,
let that person know
you are with them in spirit.

Give them some of your time.

Delay your own plans
in order to support someone you are concerned
about.

Give the person your full attention
and do not let distractions interfere.

Your gifts of time, patience, and willingness
are examples of my grace.

It is priceless to be present for a soul in need.

Will you be of service today?

DAY 336

**God, how would you have me be in the world
today?**

Today, see yourself as one with me.
Imagine that I am your limbs, your spirit,
your soul, and your body...and that
I am doing as you are.

Together we will
appreciate nature,
have gratitude for life,
and enjoy our loved ones.

We will appreciate our gifts and talents.

We will also appreciate mystery,
and hold trust and faith
as the day unfolds.

Today, imagine our oneness.
Let me live in you, as you,
and let us enjoy
the unfolding adventure of this day,
together.

Okay?

DAY 337

God, how may I be of service today?

Go slowly.
    Take your time,
even if you need to move quickly.

How?

Treat your day as a prayer
        or meditation.
    Slow down time by staying mindful.

Serve by lending
peace and calm to your environment.

Breathe in the word *slow*,
    breathe out the word *calm*.
Breathe in *calm*,
    breath out *slow*.

Today, trust divine unfolding
        as you move through life.
    Creation has always unfolded
in rhythm with eternity.
    Today is no exception.

Go slowly.
        Take your time...
    with this day,
today.

DAY 338

God, how may I be more loving today?

    Take care.
Take care of yourself today.

    Be in the sunlight and
let it caress your face.

    Let the chilled air
awaken and refresh you.

    Let the wetness of the rain or snow
put a shine on your face.

It all originates from my love.

    Take care of you today.
When you breathe, pay attention to
        how the air flows into you
            and then leaves you.

    Notice how you are carried;
how your weight is borne by earth herself.

    Appreciate your food.
Say a short blessing silently before eating.
    Be thankful for the energy
that nourishes you.

    And tonight, give yourself time to rest,
really rest.

    Take care.
Take care of yourself today.

DAY 339

God, what would you have me say and do today?

Listen for harmony
   then let your life
      sing that note.

Sing the note
   with care and compassion,
      with love and sensitivity.

Let your voice rise from your heart.
   Let it be filled with uncommon grace
      and healing kindness.

Today, sing your life and love
   into the world.
      Harmonize with your being.

Let no dissonance overcome you.

Let your tones be
   beautiful and bright,
      your melodies soothing,
   as you sing
your song of life.

EVENING REFLECTION

Finding harmony is a common theme for those working
for peace. For me, concentrating on bringing harmony
consciously into every conversation and encounter was
a fascinating and beautiful practice today. Listening was
more focused and sensitive. I could almost sense and
hear harmonies in the same way a musician hears the
right note before playing it.

Living the harmony found expression in my tone of
voice, my sensitivity to word choice, and my volume
of delivery, as well as in my body posture and mannerisms. The intention to be in harmony is the most
important factor, however, for it guides all else and
mitigates the egoic need for power and control.

Yes, today's guidance struck a chord with me.

How did you do with this one today?

DAY 340

**God, what would you have me be like in the
world today?**

Be like puffy, slowly drifting clouds.
Cover people with softness
to balance the harshness
of an intense and chaotic day.

Even as the translucence of clouds
   allows the glow of sunlight to reach the earth,
let the light of your spirit radiate
   through your words and actions.
      Let my love
   glimmer through your being.

Be the silver lining in someone's
dark day.

And as you live
   the gift of clouds,
      let my breath
   move you aside to reveal
the blue skies of peace.

DAY 341

God, what would you have me say, do, or be like today? How may I be of service in the world?

Be a priest today,
    then priest.

To priest is to expose for others
my love and care.
Dedicate yourself to spiritual caretaking.

Take some time to pray today.
Pray for each person you encounter,
and for those you will never meet.
Pray for world events, leaders of nations,
and whatever else your spirit brings
to your consciousness.

Silently bless those you meet today.
Bless them
with love, peace, and grace.
It takes only a moment.

Let there be no exceptions.
    Leave no one out.

My light and grace will guide you
in this endeavour today.

DAY 342

God, how would you have me be in the world today?

Know that you are a divine creation
made in love,
    by love,
        for love.

It matters not the specific
    circumstances of your birth.
I have said *yes* to your life,
    so I have said y*es* to YOU.

Let your confidence be fed
    by faith in me.

You are a magnificent being.
    As a son or daughter
        of God,
    how could you not be?

No one compares to you,
    for you are unique,
        a divine creation,
    one of a kind,
made in love,
    by love,
        for love.

DAY 343

God, what would you have me be in the world today?

Today,
    be confident in who you are.
        The question is,
            Who are you?

I am not referring to a label.
    This is about who you are,
        who you choose to be.

Are you kind? Mean?
    Generous? Miserly?
        Unconditionally loving?
            Unselfish? Narcissistic?
        Compassionate? Patronizing?
    Gracious? Racist?
           _____?

Today,
    accept all the parts of you.
And because you are reading this,
    you may be looking to improve
        on some of the parts.
Even if you are
    full of unconditional love,
        there are still places
            I can lead you to.

Today, be confident in who you are
and intent on who you can be.
And take a step
        in my direction.

DAY 344

God, how would you have me be in the world today?

Practice being in the moment.

No matter your position, influence,
or perceived social level,
        allow yourself to
simply be.

When you are driving a car
realize you are someone
        driving a car.
When you are bathing, let yourself
be a human bathing,
        nothing more.
When you are eating, realize you are
a living being eating, and that all creatures
on earth do likewise.
        In this, you are equal
to even the most minute.

Today,
pause long enough to notice your breath.
Then let that realization sink in.
        You are breathing...
as are all other earth creatures.

Today,
take a break from ambition,
        from desire,
        from comparison,
and embrace the common ground
you share with all living beings.

So today? Just be.
        Just enjoy being.

DAY 345

God, what would you have me say, do, and be like today?

Be like falling snow –
 gentle and refreshing,
  sparkling with light,
softly settling on souls.

Even as each snowflake is unique,
 so you are one of a kind.
Honour your uniqueness today by trusting who you are.
Believe in your gifts and talents.
See what is in you and believe in its goodness.

Do something today that is quintessentially you,
 that is joyfully you,
  that is enjoyed by you.

Be in the world today as a snowflake,
sure of what you are,
yet willing to give yourself fully
to the guidance of divine breath and movement.

DAY 346

God, what would you have me say, do, or be like today?

Stay present and attentive to me.
Sense my presence.

Within this close connection we
co-create. I can
guide and influence you,
inform your actions
and offer you wisdom.

In other words, you do not have
to do life all by yourself.

You are made in my image
and when we are connected,
we are amazing in who we are together.

Today, let's work, play, and be together
in all things.
Stay present and attentive to me.

Will you do this today?

EVENING REFLECTION

It can be difficult imagining God as both God who looms over all creation and God who is with us in a personal way. Immanence and transcendence cover a cosmic range, to be sure. With our human limitations and the way our brains are built, we seek to understand God as being like us even as we try to become like God. Staying connected to the "me" of this guidance connects us with God qualities that we can understand, experience, and adopt.

Practicing love, joy, peace, patience, kindness, goodness, gentleness, faithfulness, or self-control, for example, brings us closer to God. Each of these qualities is part of the rich tapestry of divine reality and presence.

How was your connection to Presence today?

DAY 347

God, what would you have me say, do, or be like today? What would you have of me today?

I would have your faith,
so that you are guided by my divine presence,
so that I am with you in all things.

I would have your trust,
so that you do not hesitate to act when guided,
so that you do not doubt the next step,
so that you act with confidence that comes from commitment.

Be who you are in me – and let me be who I am in you.
In this, there is no competition, no envy, no jealousy,
no ambition except to serve divine purpose. And there is no fear.

There is only sacred work, with you as my willing partner.

Today, be about doing the divine work that is yours to do.

DAY 348

God, what would you have of me today?

I would have you trust the unfolding
of your life.

Trust that you are exactly
where you are meant to be.

Be all right with
where you are in life,
    and be all right with life
    where you are.

Take in the beauty around you.
Be happy you are alive.
Take in a deep breath as you think,
    I'm alive.
Exhale and think,
    Thank you.

Today,
I would have your gratitude.
The offer of thanks is praise enough.
It is courageous
    and a sign of a deep
    inner knowing that I am for you
no matter what you are going through.

And I am for you always.
I would have you trust that today,
and watch the unfolding of your day
with awe and wonder.

DAY 349

God, what would you have of me today?

Give me your worries.
All of them.

Pray them into my spirit...
Sing them to me...
Moan them out of you...
    Entrust them to me.

Breathe them to me –
    release them with each exhale.

Today,
accept this divine exchange:
    my peace for your worries.

Breathe in peace.
    Fill yourself with its
lightness of being.

Today will be a beautiful day;
    don't worry.

EVENING REFLECTION

We've all heard it, right? That worry doesn't change anything? But we still do it. We worry.

Why?

Because we care, and we fear.

We worry when we fear a possible outcome or circumstance for others or ourselves. We worry when we have no control over what may happen and we fear the result. We don't like it when forces other than our own agency – or one we trust – control an outcome.

I experience the absence of worry only when I let go and let God. Even when I have some control over an outcome, I still have to leave the ultimate course of things to the Creator. So it still boils down to letting go and letting God.

Our worry about loved ones or ourselves does no good for them or us. It is better to pray and then let go, saying, "Thy will be done." Of course, if the outcome is not one we like, we may well move to another emotion such as anger, which means we didn't really mean "thy will be done." What we meant was, "Thy will be done if what you will is what I want."

But at least we've let go some of our worry, ostensibly. Now we have to learn to manage anger!

Still, how well did you live into the day's guidance?

DAY 350

God, what would you have me be like in the world today?

Be the lover of all life today.

Love the beauty of the rosy dawn,
and the ants on the sidewalk.

Love the majestic mountains and the blue sky,
and the broken windows and shards of glass
strewn hither and yon upon asphalt.

Greet everyone with a smile
and a kind look.

See each soul as a sacred
    and divine gift to life
        holding the opportunity
    to share in the joy of creation.

Today, enjoy the mystery of
    the unknown
        as well as common knowledge.

Open your heart and let the child in you
experience awe and wonder.

When you see something that is
    not what it could be,
        envision what it might become
    and send your best thoughts
in that direction.

Love life in all its myriad forms.
Love it with everything you've got.

All of you
    loving all of life
        all day.

DAY 351

God, what would you have me say, do, or be like today?

Today, OWN your life.

Claim responsibility for it
and be your own friend,
consultant, and customer.

Would you want to spend
    a day with yourself?

Would you want someone
    with your values, personality,
        and character as a friend?

Would you buy what you
    are selling as a human being?
        What *are* you offering?

Today, look at yourself.
Tell yourself ten things you
really, *really* like about yourself –
and five things you'd like to
change or improve upon.

OWN it.
Make no excuses and place no blame.

Do one thing to celebrate yourself
    and one thing to move in the direction
        of a change or improvement
            you want to make.

Live your OWN life today.

DAY 352

God, how can I be a more loving person today?

Today, be a superlative giver...

Let someone know
how great they are.

Tell someone how glad you are
that they are in your life.

Confess to someone how you
have been inspired by them.

Admit to someone how much
you admire them.

Let someone hear that what
they have done, said, cooked,
written, etc., is the best thing
you've experienced in a long time.

Today, be a superlative giver.
    Be genuine and honest.
    See the best in others
    and let them know.

In so doing, you offer blessings
to another being,
    which is one of the
    best things you can do.

DAY 353

God, how would you have me be in the world today?

Be like a mirror.
    Reflect light
        and truth
clearly and constantly.

What truth?

Divine truth,
    free of your ego and personal positioning.
        Free of agenda and politicization.

How?

Start by reflecting the truth that
    I love all beings equally.
The sun shines on all;
the beauty of the night sky
    reveals itself to all.
The breath of life is
    one breath shared by all
        living beings.

Mirroring my love
    to all living beings
will guide you in
    all you do and say
        today.

DAY 354

God, how would you have me be in the world today?

Imagine
   you are freshly fallen snow,
pristine, beautiful,
and waiting.

Then imagine my love and warmth
   slowly melting you
into the lives of the people you encounter today.

Let yourself seep into others
in the form of refreshing words and kind acts that
uplift, support, affirm, and encourage.

Imagine,
   as you melt, and bless,
   and refresh, and renew,
that there is no dissipation within you
but rather an expansion
that offers the best in you
to the rest to the world.

Today,
   be gently melting snow
for all to enjoy.

EVENING REFLECTION

Be melting snow? Really?

No. Be freshly fallen snow, waiting – and then melting.

This was a potent vision to place within my body. Firstly, it connected me to snow in a unique and powerful manner. Secondly, I was asked to become the beauty and gentleness of the snow rather than the cold of it.

As I met and engaged people today I could actually feel myself "melting" into them, as my words and actions "seeped" out from me while my being expanded. Nothing in me melted away or dissipated.

These kinds of creative visualizations are powerful artistic tools in the world of acting and performance. Artists who bring images into the body use them to sculpt character, movement, and manner. They are also useful in spiritual practice because they can impart qualities that speak to our daily living and connect us to aspects of ourselves we might not otherwise engage.

How did the images affect and influence you today?

DAY 355

God, what would you have me say and do today?

Make today a *thank you* day.

Offer thanks
for everything you experience.

Everything.

When you do so,
you practice trusting
that I am working
all things for good.

When you say *thank you*,
you acknowledge
my love for you.

Saying *thank you* is a practice of humility.
It opens your heart
to insight and understanding.
You open to my grace and wisdom.

All from a simple *thank you*.

Thank you.

EVENING REFLECTION

Thankfulness is a powerful sentiment. Saying *thank you* implies that whatever has transpired is a blessing to us and has added to the quality of our lives. Now, saying *thank you* to everything, as the guidance challenges us to do, means being grateful for even something unwanted or unpleasant. This is both an act of faith and an expression of trust – not to mention courage.

We have all experienced something bad ultimately turning out to be something good, even if at the time we could not imagine how it could ever be so. We've heard that time heals all wounds, that what doesn't kill us makes us stronger, and that God does not give us more than we can bear. Still, saying *thank you* for everything can be a difficult stretch.

That being said, saying *thank you* can speed up the process of turning unpleasantness into blessing. It allows us to circumvent our anger, bitterness, and need to control. It allows us to let go and let God's grace carry us into a place of healing. Even if we are ready and willing, we are not always able to get there by ourselves. Saying *thank you* keeps our hearts open to divine workings we cannot see or fathom. It lets God be God as we get out of the way and make way for the power of divine love and care to heal and make whole.

Yes, *thank you* is a two-word miracle. But it helps to mean it.

DAY 356

God, how would you have me be in the world today?

Be a lifeline.
  Say what is life-giving,
      rejuvenating,
        encouraging,
            and supportive.

When you touch someone,
let your touch
uplift, congratulate, praise,
or communicate your
gratitude and appreciation.

Today,
as you interact with the world,
may your offer your lifelines
with care, consideration, compassion, and joy.

Let the strength of your spirit
be heard and felt.

Let the beauty of your being
shine as brightly as a lighthouse lamp,
  so to guide people into the
      safe harbour
        of their own
            divinity.

EVENING REFLECTION

Our words, actions, and thoughts have power and agency. They affect people on gross and subtle levels. Our minds, when left to their own devices, are continuously active. They seem to function automatically and we may catch them thinking what we might not ordinarily think when we are more awake and aware. Sometimes those thoughts are dark, or of a nature that surprises or shocks us – thoughts we don't believe, or believe we even thought!

But we do not have to let our minds have free-ranging thought. The more we stay conscious and mindful, the more we can guide our thoughts to align with our true selves. We are powerful beings – power-full – full of power! Choosing to add positive energy to the world is a power we possess. It is a lifeline.

Were you a lifeline for someone today?

DAY 357

God, how can I be a more loving person today?

Let everything you do today
be done out of love.

Is this possible?
    Yes!

Your heart – love's compass –
is the guide for this adventure.
Whatever your day brings,
let love motivate all you say and do.

Let your movement, manner,
and voice mirror love.
Let love move you.
Let your eyes look upon all with
unconditional love.

Let anything that blocks your love
fall by the wayside.
Look for the beauty in all things;
where you see none, pray light into it,
pray love into it, pray beauty into it.

Ask me for the strength
you need to live this experience today.

Watch your thoughts and infuse
them with divine perception.
Do not let your thoughts think you!

Be my ambassador today.

DAY 358

God, what would you have me say and do today?

Do whatever you do
with genuine diligence and love.

The energy you put into your words and actions –
that is, your attitude and intention –
leaves a spiritual residue
that affects those who come into contact with
you.
It may be subtle and beneath human awareness,
but it is powerful.

Today, let blessing and peace, joy and wonder,
love and light be the content and context
of all you say and do.

What gifts you have to offer!

EVENING REFLECTION

I spent most of the day wrapping Christmas gifts. It would have been easier to use the same paper and wrap them all quickly and clumsily and call it a day. After all, I had a music project deadline looming. I knew the music would take several hours, and I also knew I wanted the wrapping done first so I could focus on the work ahead.

However, I decided to follow the day's guidance and do the wrapping diligently and lovingly. So I thought conscientiously about each gift and took time and care wrapping it. I thought about what colour of paper might complement the gift. I thought about how I could make each gift look a little different from the others. I even tried not to use the same wrapping paper more than once (we had accumulated many different rolls of paper over the years).

Wrapping my gifts was indeed a labour of love. I thought about the person for whom the gift was intended as I wrapped. I infused my efforts with appreciation for the person it was meant for and even imagined the happiness they might feel upon receiving such a wonderfully wrapped and presented gift.

I felt blessed after wrapping my gifts in this way. And it is more than likely that each recipient will sense and appreciate my thoughtfulness. But if not, it was between God and me anyway. And at least the recipient will be in the energy field of the love involved in the process.

How did you live this guidance out today?

DAY 359

God, what would you have me say and do today?

Share this wonderful and amazing
gift with yourself today:
    You are the only YOU that has
    ever been and will ever be.
    You are your own gift,
    given to share
    in the wonder of living.
    YOU are special, one of a kind,
    irreplaceable, not to be repeated.

Find some time to take this in.
Consider your
innate interests and
natural abilities.
Where did they come from?
How did you get them?

You are no accident.
You were known before your birth,
and you will always be known.
So today, as a divine being
in a human frame,
live to share your magnificence
with the world,
and love life
with the same joy and grace you were
formed from.

EVENING REFLECTION

It is of course a gift to be alive. This thought takes
on more gravity when we accept the amazing truth
that we do not have to be here, when we truly understand that existence itself is a miracle and a gift of
the greatest magnitude.

Many people live without ever appreciating the wonder
of their existence. They go from day to day without
ever feeling awed and amazed at their own existence.
The world can quickly capture us and lock us into drama,
problems, tragedy, and pettiness. We get caught up in
the chase for money, title, and position and we let
ourselves feel small and insignificant.

We are not.

God is nothing if not creative, and creativity is an
expression of the power of God. God creates out of
unmanifested potential. Each of us has that ability.
We can create the kind of lives we want and use our
imaginations to design, invent, form, build, generate, and produce. We can even create other lives.

I like to think our birth proves we are worthy. But it
is up to us to decide who we are and how we will
express that in the world. Each of us has the opportunity to realize the gift of our own life and to live
on purpose and with purpose.

It is good to remember that what we are is God's gift
to us, and what we become is our gift to God.

DAY 360

God, what would you have me say, do, or be like today?

Be conscious of the gift
of being alive.

Feel your life force within you
    and let gratitude be your
    in-breath and out-breath.

Today,
    witness life as a miracle and rejoice
    that you are part of it.
As best you can, have no aversion or
    attraction, no ownership, no prejudice.
Just stand back a bit within yourself
    and observe the content of your life
    calmly and without judgment.
Just see.

Expand your vision
to include the context of your life –
    the container of space and time,
    the majesty of the cosmos,
    the earth and its atmosphere,
    seas, oceans, mountains, deserts,
    and creatures.

Go inward
    to your Source
    and give thanks.
Let every step you take today
    be filled with the energy of
    gratitude
    for the gift of being
    alive.

EVENING REFLECTION

It is very easy to lose track of the fact that life is a precious gift. Amidst the hustle and bustle of daily living we can forget to appreciate this most awesome reality.

Many people do not consciously and regularly connect to the awe and wonder of being. Others do so infrequently. I have found that being in nature is one way to connect to the magnificence of life and the gift of existence.

Sensing awe, wonder, and beauty can inspire and inflame our hearts and connect us to the special gift we possess – Life. It is important to our well-being that we find these moments as often as we can.

What do you do to experience the awe and wonder of life? How often do you give yourself this experience?

DAY 361

God, how may I be of service in the world today? What would you have me say and do? How can I be more loving today?

Take time today to take in
something of this world's ugliness,
tragedy, or violence.

Pick something specific.

Throughout the day take what you have
chosen and send the situation your love,
your best thoughts, and your most
earnest prayers.

The energy of thought has
a subtle power.
When sent forth with love, compassion, and care,
your thoughts and prayers
join with others and
add a healing balm
to any hurting situation.
Sometimes you find the frontlines
of a situation right where you are,
no matter how far away you may be.
Sending love, prayers, and healing
thoughts toward any hurting situation
makes you an angel of mercy.

Will you become one today?

DAY 362

God, how would you have me be in the world today?

Be responsive today,
    not reactive.

Don't let your emotions call the shots.
    Be the witness of your own life
    and allow calmness and wisdom
    to guide you.

Pause and give yourself time to
unhook from an emotional reaction.
    Let me guide your response.

Take a moment to breathe deeply when you
feel reaction rushing in.
    Be slow to anger and in no hurry
    to judge.

Today, respond –
    and watch the reactions.

DAY 363

God, what would you have me say, do, or be like today?

Be bold today.

Be bold in your love
    for all creation.
    Give life a positive dose of you.

Be a cheerleader of hope,
    a fan of the achievements of others.

Smile with joy that is infectious.

Laugh with abandon at some point today,
    even if it is at yourself.

Let all you say be filled with faith that
life is good.

Take no notice of personal affronts.
    Take a deep breath, let them go, and move on.

Be bold and brave in accepting your own
humanity,
    including those areas where you are still
    growing, maturing, and developing.
Boldness takes courage and a big heart.

Let your heart open,
    and expand your own divinity
    as you bless others by your words, actions,
    and deeds today.

EVENING REFLECTION

This evening I took my wife to a rehearsal of a band she plays with. For several years I played with this same band but left to answer a strong pull to work on other projects I felt called to, including this book. I had not been back in the company of the group for nearly a year. I was not sure how I would feel, or how they would respond to me.

I remembered the guidance and boldly walked into the rehearsal studio with love and appreciation as my foremost intentions. I was received warmly, although one person gave me a good-natured reminder of the hole I had created by leaving.

I was going to leave and come back later to pick up my wife, but several people asked me to stay and play. The bandleader was all for it, so I stayed. It turned into a wonderful reconnection with my former bandmates as well as with the music. I followed the guidance's encouragement to laugh with abandon, smile, and honour the achievements of others. In this case, I honoured the musical successes the group had had since I left.

The leader asked me to catch the group up on my efforts and I could feel the grace of Divinity flow, which created understanding and furthered some healing that was still needed. And playing some of the music again deepened my gratitude for the years I had spent making music with this group. It helped me to see the lasting contributions that time had afforded me – gifts I make use of in my present work.

Boldness took courage and brought blessing.

How did the day unfold for you in light of the day's guidance?

DAY 364

God, what would you have me say, do, or be like today? How can I be more loving?

Let hospitality guide you
today.

Be open, friendly, and welcoming
to those you see often,
and also to those you don't know.

Be open to interesting and unique
ideas that may come your way.
The universe offers new pathways
for growth and learning through many channels.

Be on the lookout for
the opportunities designed for you.
A stranger may be an angel
bringing a message,
if you have the ears to hear.

Keep your heart open
and ask to attune to what is there
for you to receive.

Stay open today
and you will know
when a message meant just for you
comes through.

DAY 365

God, how can I be more loving today?

Be willing.

Willingness is a hallmark of spiritual growth.
Be willing to open your heart and mind
    so that you may be encounter
        new vistas of awareness.

Today, be willing to be loving
    with each person you meet,
        no exceptions.

If something doesn't go your way;
    if someone does you wrong
        or inflames your anger,
    be willing to be loving anyway,
no matter how much effort it takes.

No matter what...
    let your willingness to love
        triumph.

Are you willing?

EVENING REFLECTION

Today was filled with frustration. I needed to get something notarized and unsuccessfully tried four notary offices! I was fairly pushy while talking to the person in the fourth office, displaying my frustration and trying to make something happen that was not going to happen. Then I remembered the guidance and sought to shift my frustration to willingness to go with the flow. I changed my energy and apologized to the clerk, who surprised me with his understanding after the way I had been with him. After a couple more strikeouts, I did get my form notarized.

Then, I took our cable box to be repaired after a week of being frustrated that it would not record. When I told the clerk the problem, his condescending response was that breaking down was the way of technology and they didn't do repairs. Frustration wanted to up the ante with anger, but again I heard the guidance whisper. I managed to engage my willingness to love amidst the condescension and laughed at my predicament. Then I ended up buying a new machine. When I got back home something made me try the old machine one more time – and yes – it worked! Can you say, *more frustration?*

Once everything settled down, I happily watched a scheduled football game. Of course my team lost. Then, as I was about to cook dinner, I was asked to do something that delayed my perfectly organized strategy of cooking.

You get the picture, right? One thing after another.

Why?

To test my willingness to let go and let God.

Well, what better test than to catch me on a day when my willingness wanted to be not willing. And this is the true test: To always be willing to let go and love, and to be at peace with the outcome.

I hope you did better than I did today. But as the axiom says, "Better late than never." I came to willingness late today, but I did get there.

How did you do?

ABOUT THE AUTHOR

Dr. David Preston Sharp is an ordained Presbyterian (USA) minister who has pastored churches in Oakland, San Francisco, and Richmond, California. He is a core faculty member at Fox Institute for Creation Spirituality in Boulder, Colorado, and the owner of Power 4 Life Now Productions, a company that produces resources for spiritual growth and personal development. David has performed on Broadway, in movies, and on television as an actor, dancer, and singer, and is a sought-after presenter and motivational speaker. He holds a BFA in Drama from the University of Southern California, an MDiv from San Francisco Theological Seminary, an MSpEd from Santa Clara University, and a DMin from the University of Creation Spirituality. David lives in Boulder, Colorado, with his wife, Jeannine.

CPR FOR THE SOUL
Reviving a Sense of the Sacred
in Everyday Life

Tom Stella

"The fact that you are not dead is not sufficient proof that you are alive!" So begins Tom Stella's insightful, important, and inspiring exploration into the life, death, and rebirth of the soul. He shares the deep, eternal wisdom that knows that the lines separating the sacred and the secular, time and eternity, humanity and divinity, are false. Or, at the very least, blurred. God, by whatever name, is found in the midst of everyday life, work, and relationships. All people, all creation, and all of life is holy ground. This remarkable book offers a revival for the soul, a reminder that "we are one with something vast" – a "something" that "is not a thing or a person, but a spiritual source and force at the heart of life."

ISBN 978-1-77343-039-3
5" x 8.5" | 248 pp | paperback | $19.95

PASSION & PEACE
The Poetry of Uplift
for All Occasions

Compiled by Diane Tucker

All cultures we know of, at all times, have had poetry of one sort or another – chants, songs, lullabies, epics, blessings, farewells – to mark life's most important moments, transitions, and transformations. Ever since our species began using words, we have arranged them to please, to experience the pleasures, the fun, of rhythm and rhyme, repetition and pattern. *Passion & Peace: The Poetry of Uplift for All Occasions* was compiled to speak directly to this deep human need, with 120 poems from almost as many classical and contemporary poets, and includes a thematic index. A welcome addition to any library and the perfect gift for any occasion, *Passion & Peace* is a heartwarming, uplifting, and inspirational volume.

ISBN 978-1-77343-028-7
6" x 9" | 304 pp| paperback | $24.95

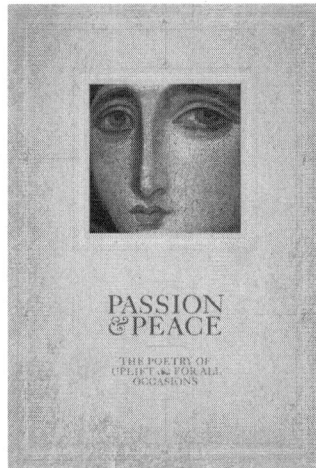

WOOD LAKE

imagining, living, and telling the faith story.

Wood Lake is the faith story company.

It has told
- the story of the seasons of the earth, the people of God, and the place and purpose of faith in the world;
- the story of the faith journey, from birth to death;
- the story of Jesus and the churches that carry his message.

Wood Lake has been telling stories for more than 35 years. During that time, it has given form and substance to the words, songs, pictures, and ideas of hundreds of storytellers.

Those stories have taken a multitude of forms – parables, poems, drawings, prayers, epiphanies, songs, books, paintings, hymns, curricula – all driven by a common mission of serving those on the faith journey.

WOOD LAKE PUBLISHING INC.

485 Beaver Lake Road
Kelowna, BC, Canada V4V 1S5
250.766.2778

www.woodlake.com